THE IMPORTANCE OF

Anwar Sadat

These and other titles are included in The Importance Of biography series:

THE IMPORTANCE OF

Anwar Sadat

by
Arthur Diamond

Lucent Books, P.O. Box 289011, San Diego, CA 92198-9011

Acknowledgments

I would like to thank the following individuals for their contributions to this book: Gary Rubin of the *Seattle Times*, Alfred and Luly Kaufman, and my editor, Bonnie Szumski.

Dedication

To the memory of my brother, Morton Allan Diamond

Library of Congress Cataloging-in-Publication Data

Diamond, Arthur.
    Anwar Sadat / by Arthur Diamond.
        p. cm.—(The Importance of)
    Includes bibliographical references (p.) and index.
    Summary: A biography of the famous Egyptian leader, tracing his rise to power, his part in the 1973 war with Israel, and his role in the peace process, which won him the Nobel Peace Prize.
    ISBN 1-56006-020-4 (alk. paper)
    1. Sadat, Anwar, 1918- —Juvenile literature. 2. Presidents—Egypt—Biography—Juvenile literature. [1. Sadat, Anwar, 1918- . 2. Presidents—Egypt.] I. Title. II. Series.
DT107.828.S23D53   1994
962.05'4'092—dc20
[B]   93-17096
                                                                                 CIP
                                                                                  AC

Copyright 1994 by Lucent Books, Inc., P.O. Box 289011, San Diego, California, 92198-9011

Printed in the U.S.A.

Contents

Foreword

THE IMPORTANCE OF biography series deals with individuals who have made a unique contribution to history. The editors of the series have deliberately chosen to cast a wide net and include people from all fields of endeavor. Individuals from politics, music, art, literature, philosophy, science, sports, and religion are all represented. In addition, the editors did not restrict the series to individuals whose accomplishments have helped change the course of history. Of necessity, this criterion would have eliminated many whose contribution was great, though limited. Charles Darwin, for example, was responsible for radically altering the scientific view of the natural history of the world. His achievements continue to impact the study of science today. Others, such as Chief Joseph of the Nez Percé, played a pivotal role in the history of their own people. While Joseph's influence does not extend much beyond the Nez Percé, his nonviolent resistance to white expansion and his continuing role in protecting his tribe and his homeland remain an inspiration to all.

These biographies are more than factual chronicles. Each volume attempts to emphasize an individual's contributions both in his or her own time and for posterity. For example, the voyages of Christopher Columbus opened the way to European colonization of the New World. Unquestionably, his encounter with the New World brought monumental changes to both Europe and the Americas in his day. Today, however, the broader impact of Columbus's voyages is being critically scrutinized. *Christopher Columbus,* as well as every biography in The Importance Of series, includes and evaluates the most recent scholarship available on each subject.

Each author includes a wide variety of primary and secondary source quotations to document and substantiate his or her work. All quotes are footnoted to show readers exactly how and where biographers derive their information, as well as provide stepping stones to further research. These quotations enliven the text by giving readers eyewitness views of the life and times of each individual covered in The Importance Of series.

Finally, each volume is enhanced by photographs, bibliographies, chronologies, and comprehensive indexes. For both the casual reader and the student engaged in research, The Importance Of biographies will be a fascinating adventure into the lives of people who have helped shape humanity's past, present, and will continue to shape its future.

Important Dates in the Life of Anwar Sadat

1918 — Anwar Sadat is born in the small village of Mit Abul-Kum on December 25.

1938 — Graduates from the Royal Military Academy; assigned to a post in Manqabad, in southern Egypt.

1940 — Helps organize the Free Officer's Association.

1941 — Arrested by the British, then freed.

1942 — Spends two years in jail for role in anti-British plot.

1946 — Arrested again—for his role in the assassination of Amin Osman Pasha; spends two more years in jail.

1948 — Freed from jail.

1949 — Sadat divorces his first wife and marries Jehan Raouf.

1952 — King Farouk is overthrown; Gamel Abdul Nasser becomes new ruler of Egypt.

1956 — Nasser nationalizes the Suez Canal; war breaks out between Egypt and the forces of Israel, France, and Britain. The allied forces eventually withdraw, leaving Egypt in control of the canal.

1967 — The Six Day War breaks out; Israel triumphs over Egypt.

1970 — Upon Nasser's death, Sadat becomes president of Egypt.

1971 — Sadat foils a coup attempt.

1972 — Sadat orders all Soviet military experts to leave Egypt.

1973 — October War begins as Sadat stages a surprise attack against Israel; within days Israel battles back, and Egypt loses the war.

1975 — Sadat reopens the Suez Canal, closed since 1967.

1977 — Anwar Sadat flies to Jerusalem to talk peace with his Israeli counterpart, Menachem Begin.

1978 — Sadat and Begin meet with U.S. president Jimmy Carter and produce the historic Camp David Accords; the Egyptian and Israeli leaders are awarded the Nobel Peace Prize.

1981 — Riots break out between Copts and Muslims in Egypt; Sadat cracks down on Muslim militants, opposition politicians, and the press; Sadat is assassinated by militant Muslims.

A Bold Move

In June 1975, the Suez Canal, Egypt's commercial waterway between the Red Sea and the Mediterranean, lay unused. Since the Israeli-Arab war of 1967, the canal had been closed. The losses to Egypt's economy had been staggering. The canal, since it had first opened in 1869, was one of the four largest sources of government income. Its closing cost Egypt hundreds of millions of dollars. And then the October War of 1973 between Israel and its Arab neighbors left the man-made canal cluttered with the rotting remains of ships and checkered with hidden mines.

The cities along the banks of the Suez Canal had long been abandoned—and for good reasons. The canal cities of Ismailia,

Israeli soldiers watch Egyptian positions on the opposite side of the Suez Canal during the Israeli-Arab war of 1967.

Anwar Sadat boldly leads a convoy of Egyptian ships down the Suez Canal during its reopening in June 1975. By opening the canal to international traffic, Sadat helped establish diplomatic relations with Israel and the world.

Port Said, and Suez were right in the line of fire of Israeli forces stationed across the canal, on the shore of the Sinai Peninsula. Israel had captured the Sinai Peninsula from Egypt in the 1967 war. Israeli guns were loaded and aimed at Egyptian batteries. Israeli planes were ready for attack. Skirmishes on both sides of the canal left each side continually prepared for any sudden outbreak of hostilities.

On the morning of June 5, 1975, a number of ships gathered on the Egyptian side of the canal. Israel watched with great interest. Over the past few months, despite the ominous presence of the Israeli mili-

tary, Egypt had undertaken a large-scale cleanup of the Suez. Israel's foremost ally, the United States, had sent troops and equipment to assist the Egyptians. American helicopters towed mine-seeking sleds over the murky canal waters, and Egyptian tugs towed away disabled ships.

Since Israel and America were friends, Israel allowed the cleanup, trusting that the United States would not endanger Israel's interests. Moreover, until that point in time, Egypt's Anwar Sadat was the only leader of the Arab world who had ever talked about peace with Israel. The Israelis were skeptical as to whether Sadat's talk would lead to a significant breakthrough. They had too often experienced the sound of Arab guns since the creation of their state.

The morning of June 5 brought a different sound. From intelligence reports, the Israelis had known for days that Egyptian ships would begin to make their way down the Suez Canal. Yet Israeli soldiers still had trouble believing that the president of Egypt, Anwar Sadat himself, was on one of the ships. However, soon it was confirmed. Dressed in a white admiral's uniform and standing on the Egyptian destroyer *October 6*, Anwar Sadat could be seen leading the convoy through the waters, in close range of Israeli guns.

Anwar Sadat had already proved to the world he was capable of taking risks. As a young man, he had fought against the British forces that had occupied Egypt. As president of Egypt, he had infuriated the Soviet Union by throwing eighteen thousand Soviet advisors out of Egypt. In the 1973 October War, he had sent forty-five thousand Egyptian soldiers up against the well-trained and well-armed Israeli military.

Now, Sadat again took a great personal

risk. He knew that he was within the target sights of many Israeli guns. Yet he stood in the open, leading the convoy, to prove a point. Since the end of the October War, the peace process between Egypt and Israel had stalled. Sadat felt he had to do something daring to get things moving again. "I took that risk . . . for the sake of peace. In the search for peace, everything is permissible."[1] The Israelis saw no reason to take advantage of Sadat's vulnerability, and the reopening of the canal proceeded without incident.

While all Egyptians were proud of their leader's courage, the 700,000 Egyptian citizens in the canal towns were the happiest. Since their president had officially reopened the canal to international traffic, they felt free to return to their homes after years of exile in Egypt's crowded cities. Sadat himself later recalled: "I shall never forget that day. The joy that lit up the eyes of men, women, and children was really beautiful. They had been repatriated at last."[2]

With this bold move, Sadat showed the Israelis and the rest of the world that rebuilding his country was more important than war. And rebuilding his country required peace. "Nothing in this world," Sadat would later say, "could rank higher than peace."[3]

1 Loving the Land, Hating the Occupiers

Anwar el-Sadat was born on December 25, 1918, in Mit Abul-Kum. This small farming village sits in the Nile Delta seventy miles northwest of Cairo, Egypt. During the first seven years of his life, young Anwar did not see much of his father, Mohammed el-Sadat. Anwar's father was a hospital clerk in the British-controlled Egyptian army and was stationed in the Sudan, the country directly south of Egypt.

Under Islamic law, men could have up to four wives at one time. Fetching water and handling household matters were traditional jobs for Egyptian wives.

Anwar's Family

Though his father was absent during the first six or seven years of his life, Anwar knew that Mohammed el-Sadat was well respected by the other villagers. Most young people dreamed of going to a religious school and becoming Muslim clerics. Mohammed el-Sadat was fortunate enough to go to such a school. He became the first person in Mit Abul-Kum to earn the General Certificate of Primary Education, a special degree. He was then known as "the effendi," a title of respect given by the peasant class to educated people or to those in the ruling class.

While Mohammed el-Sadat was away, Anwar's grandmother, Om Mohammed ("Mother of Mohammed"), took charge of the family and moved them into her house. Because Anwar's mother, Sit el-Barrein, was a guest in the new house, she had to not interfere in household matters, along with Amina, Mohammed's other

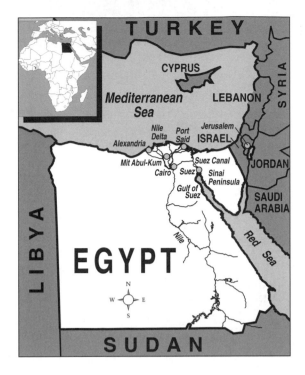

Schooling

With encouragement from his grand-mother, Anwar entered El Kottab, the village school. There he learned to read and write Arabic, as well as study the Koran, Islam's holy book. One teacher, Sheikh Abdul-Hamid, made a lasting impression on Anwar. "He was the first to instill in me the love of learning and the spirit of true faith,"[5] Anwar later said.

Young Anwar was a devout student. Like the other boys in the school (girls were not admitted), he was required to memorize all 114 chapters of the Koran and pray often. He developed what was called a "prayer knot": a callous in the center of the forehead created by regularly touching the forehead to a mat in prayer. This was the beginning of religion as an important force in Anwar's life.

Love of the Country

While he enjoyed his time in school, Anwar also enjoyed the simple delights of village life. He liked to slip an onion into the oven in the morning beside the baking bread. Later in the day he would remove the onion and feast on it. He treasured fresh molasses and would mix it with curdled milk.

As a boy, Anwar longed to be out in the Egyptian countryside, which he considered "a series of uninterrupted pleasures."[6] Watching the villagers working out in the fields, selling fresh produce in the markets, or herding their livestock home at dusk, Anwar strongly felt he was a part of the land: "It was that feeling that

wife. (Under Islamic law, men could have up to four wives at the same time. During the course of his life Mohammed el-Sadat would have eight wives and father thirteen children.)

Though illiterate like most of the other villagers, Om Mohammed was a powerful person and respected by many. Other villagers were in awe of her ability to heal the sick with special medicines she derived from herbs. Villagers with personal problems would come and consult her for advice. When she walked down a narrow street or lane in Mit Abul-Kum men came up to her and politely greeted her. This show of respect, which was not ordinarily shown to women, impressed young Anwar. Om Mohammed proved to be a tough businesswoman, too, when she took charge of her husband's farm after he died. "How I loved that woman,"[4] Anwar later said in tribute.

made me, on the way home at sunset, gaze at the evening scene with a rare warmth, recognizing an invisible bond of love and friendship with everything around me—the smoke rolling down the valley promising a delicious meal at the close of a village day, and a perfect calm and peace in the hearts of all."[7]

Heroes and Villains

Stories of Egyptian patriots and heroes told by the village elders instilled a sense of pride in young Anwar. One popular story was that of Zahran, the Egyptian martyr. Zahran was a villager in the nearby village of Denshway. One day, British soldiers shooting at pigeons accidentally shot a silo filled with wheat and set it ablaze. When local villagers tried to put out the fire, a British soldier shot at them. The villagers chased the soldier, and he was killed in the scuffle that followed.

The British took immediate revenge. Even before holding trials to determine who was guilty of shooting the soldier, they erected scaffolds and began hanging villagers. Zahran was the first to be hanged. Stories were told of his courage and how he walked proudly and unafraid to the scaffold. The heroic tale led Anwar to feel a smoldering hatred for the British. "Even before I saw the British, I had learned to hate the aggressors who whipped and killed our people."[8]

The villagers told other stories of British brutality. In one, the British poisoned Mustafa Kamil, an Egyptian political leader, because they wanted to get rid of the man who opposed their occupation. "I did not know at the time who Mustafa Kamil was or that he actually died in his prime. I knew only, at that tender age, that there were forces, called 'the British,' who were alien to us, and that they were evil because they poisoned people."[9]

Egypt's history is marked by long periods of foreign domination. The British, for example, remained in control of Egypt from 1882 until the 1950s. Pictured are British troops in Cairo, Egypt's capital city, in 1882.

The Family Furn

Jehan Sadat, in her book, A Woman of Egypt, *recalls the tenderness with which her husband used to tell her of his days growing up in Mit Abul-Kum:*

"At night, he loved to tell me later, he would lie on the top of the high family furn, a primitive oven enclosed in a bench of dried mud, eat the onion he had left to roast in it all day, and listen to his mother and grandmother tell bedtime stories of modern Egyptian heroes standing up to the British. So much did he love this warm moment of the day that later, when he would build our own home in Mit Abul-Kum, Anwar would insist on having a traditional mud furn alongside our more modern gas oven."

A History of Occupation

Whether from the village or the city, every Egyptian learns at an early age of Egypt's long history of domination by outside nations. Libyan and Syrian rulers, as well as Greek and Roman, all had dominated ancient Egypt at one time or another. The Arab invasion of A.D. 641 turned Egypt into a province of the Arab empire. In the centuries that followed, Egypt continued to fall under the rule of outside nations, including the Mamluks and the Ottoman Turks.

By the latter part of the nineteenth century, European interests dominated Egypt. In 1876, after the financially irresponsible Egyptian leader Ismail was unable to keep Egypt from bankruptcy, the British and French were called in to take charge of the country's economy. A few years later, British troops defeated an uprising of Egyptian army officers and began their occupation of the land. The British forces claimed they would make Egypt politically and economically stable.

In reality, British rule only benefitted the well-to-do upper classes, with whom the occupying British soldiers and administrators felt a kinship. The general mass of Egyptians continued their centuries-long suffering. No one was fooled in 1922 when Britain declared Egypt an independent monarchy. Though Egyptian revolutionaries pressured the British to leave Egypt and allow it to develop as its own sovereign nation, the new ruler, King Fuad, was under the control of the British. And so was Egypt's economy, military, and foreign policy.

To the City

In 1925—three years after the beginning of King Fuad's reign—village life ended for seven-year-old Anwar. Once again, the conflict between Egypt and its British oc-

Ahmed Fuad took the title of king when Britain declared Egypt an independent monarchy in 1922. King Fuad, however, remained under the control of the British. For many, living conditions deteriorated under Fuad's reign.

cupiers profoundly affected the young boy. In 1924, Sir Lee Stack, a British official serving in the Sudan, was assassinated. In retaliation for the killing, the British sent back to Egypt the Egyptian army sta-

tioned in the Sudan. Mohammed el-Sadat returned, along with the rest of the Egyptian soldiers, and found work in Cairo, Egypt's capital city. He then sent for his family to join him.

Living conditions for Anwar and his family were worse in Cairo than they had been in Mit Abul-Kum. Anwar, his two brothers Esmat and Talaat, his sister Nefisa, and his mother and father all shared a four-room apartment. Soon, they were joined by Mohammed's second wife, Amina, and the children she bore. Eventually, there were thirteen children, along with the adults, living in the four rooms. Hunger was a constant companion, for Mohammed el-Sadat had only a modest salary. At lunchtime at school, young Anwar would often spend his entire daily allowance of 2 millimes—a very small sum—on a large glass of milky tea.

Struggling Through School

Although Anwar and his brother Talaat were admitted to secondary school after completing primary school, coming up with the tuition money presented a problem. For both boys, the school would cost Mohammed el-Sadat one month's salary. During the first month of school, Anwar's father gave Anwar and his brother the money for school. Anwar paid his tuition, but Talaat took the money and ran away. Talaat spent the money and returned a few days later, declaring he would not continue his schooling. This was lucky for Anwar, who was ready to quit school because of their father's financial burden in sending both boys to school.

Other students in the secondary

school showed no such problems with money. A few of Anwar's fellow students—children of the upper class—rode to school in limousines and wore beautiful clothes. While Anwar went hungry most of the day, other, wealthier students snacked on expensive chocolates.

Anwar, though, was not impressed with those who had more wealth than he had. He felt proud of his village and especially of his ties to the land. He did not wish to have what anyone else had. One day, Anwar went into a store and asked for "mutches" instead of "matches." The shopkeeper and some customers made fun of him for mispronouncing the common word. But Anwar was not hurt. "I became obstinate and realized that I felt stronger than them. Who did they think they were? How could they justify their derision?"[10] Even at this early age, Anwar understood that integrity was a person's most important possession.

More Heroes

While he would never lose his love for Zahran, Anwar came to idolize a new set of heroes. One of them was Adolf Hitler. In 1930, three years before he would come to power and begin to commit monstrous crimes upon the world, Hitler and his Nazi gangs marched from Munich to Berlin to protest Germany's deterioration since World War I.

The twelve-year-old Sadat was impressed with the way Hitler had thwarted authority to protest something he believed in. He also appreciated the fact that Hitler was an enemy of the British. So when young Anwar was back in the village of Mit Abul-Kum for summer vacation, he told his friends they should follow Hitler's example and march from the village all the way to Cairo. The response of his friends, however, was disappointing. "They laughed and went away."[11]

Sadat's passion for heroes did not end with childhood. Hitler would hold a special fascination for him—even as late as 1953. As author Patricia Aufderheide reported, when Sadat was a member of the ruling Revolutionary Command Council

Despite strong ties to village life, Anwar's family moved to the bustling city of Cairo, where Mohammed el-Sadat found work. Here, the family lived in cramped quarters and often went hungry.

Mohandas Gandhi—who practiced nonviolent civil disobedience—was an inspiration to young Anwar. In tribute to the Indian leader, Anwar went on a hunger strike to protest British occupation of Egypt.

dience. In doing so, he not only succeeded in getting the British to improve conditions for the Indian people, but he was also admired by people all over the world. Gandhi's passive defiance of British rule eventually resulted in the emancipation of India after World War II.

When Gandhi visited Egypt in 1932 on his way to England, fourteen-year-old Anwar, having read newspaper and magazine accounts of the great man's visit, reacted strongly. He wrapped himself in a robe on a chilly afternoon and climbed to the roof of his parents' house in Cairo. There—in tribute to Gandhi—he refused all food and would not talk to anyone. Anwar's father finally persuaded the boy to come down, stating that he would only catch pneumonia, and what good would that do in ridding Egypt of the British?

The Royal Military Academy

In 1936, Sadat received his General Certificate of Primary Education, which was the equivalent of a high school diploma. A great opportunity arose, as the Egyptian government, with the assent of the British, had recently opened up officer training at the Royal Military Academy to young Egyptians from the lower classes. Until recently, only upper class Egyptians from families with land and business interests were allowed to become army officers. This was because the British believed that only those from wealthy families had an interest in protecting the pro-British government.

Anwar was able to get into the academy through his father's army friend, who was working in the government office

after the ouster of King Farouk, "he wrote favorably of Adolf Hitler, whom he praised for challenging Britain and restoring national pride."[12] That year, Sadat also wrote a fan letter to Hitler, who was believed by some to still be alive and in hiding.

A Tribute to Gandhi

Young Sadat also learned of and revered the great Indian leader, Mohandas Gandhi. In opposing British rule in his country, Gandhi practiced nonviolent civil disobe-

The Importance of the Village

Camelia Sadat, one of Anwar Sadat's daughters from his first marriage, wrote in her book, My Father and I, *of her father's connection to village life:*

"The village itself was also a lasting model for my father. The agrarian life of the village stressed the interdependence of members of the community. Without the aid and psychological support of friends and neighbors, survival for a family would be difficult. The coming together of community members of work and for special observances such as weddings and funerals constituted a continuing affirmation of that interdependence. That mutual reliance and strength of village life became a theme in Anwar's later political speeches, in which he often referred to Egypt as a large village. And as president, he would hear complaints from the students at Cairo University with the patience, skill, and humor of a village omda, or mayor."

where military academy applications were reviewed. Anwar went with his father to the man's home, where the pasha (Turkish for "lord") was nowhere to be found. Sadat and his father waited patiently in a hallway. Finally the pasha rushed down the hall and stopped before them. The busy pasha addressed them abruptly and, without any attempt to be friendly, signed the necessary papers and sent the two away.

Sadat was terribly offended. He did not like being treated as if he and his father were of no importance. He resolved that some day he would show this man that he, too, could be important. Thirty years later, when Sadat was the speaker of the National Assembly, Sadat encountered the man again. This time, it was the official who needed something from Sadat— some help resolving a property dispute. Sadat reminded the man of the meeting years before and declared, "I owe you a lot. If it hadn't been for you, the revolution wouldn't have been possible."[13]

Chapter
2 Cell 54

In late 1938 Anwar Sadat graduated from the Royal Military Academy's shortened nine-month officer course. As a second lieutenant in the infantry, Sadat pondered independence for Egypt. He decided, finally, that the only way to get the British out of Egypt was by force. He also decided that it was up to the Egyptian military to move the British out of Egypt. Anwar developed a bold plan: He wanted to organize Egyptian officers against their British commanders.

Sadat Meets Nasser

Stationed in a small town called Manqabad in the south of Egypt, Sadat met another officer, Gamal Abdel Nasser. Nasser was one of a handful of men who came to Sadat's room to smoke pipes and discuss politics and Egyptian history. Like Sadat, Gamal Abdel Nasser had been born and raised in a small village. He was also an imposing figure, who, as author Peter Woodward explained, was "Tall and well-built . . . [with] a physical presence backed by a seriousness and intensity of purpose."[14]

Nasser was also not given to communicating freely, as Sadat soon realized: "He listened to our conversations with interest

Anwar Sadat as a second lieutenant after graduating from the Royal Military Academy in 1938.

but rarely opened his mouth."[15] Still the intense young villager won the respect of his comrades, including Sadat, who came to call Nasser "the teacher," a term of respect in Muslim societies. Sadat and Nasser became friends, especially because they shared the same strong contempt for the British occupation of Egypt.

In the Shadow of War

In 1939, Germany invaded Poland. France and Britain then declared war on Germany, and World War II began. Even though Egyptians were technically subjects of Britain and therefore part of the war, Egyptians did not feel supportive of the British cause. In fact, just the opposite was true: Egyptians saw themselves as the victims of British colonialism, and Italy and Germany might be able to help liberate them.

As Britain and France battled the Nazis in Europe, Sadat planned for a revolution in Egypt. In 1939, he was sent from Manqabad north to Maadi, near Cairo, to train Maadi troops in army signals. The system of army signals is part of the intricate communications network used by military forces.

Sadat used the opportunity to make contacts with many junior and senior officers stationed in Maadi and nearby Cairo. He and other officers formed the secret Free Officer's Association. The supreme goal of the association was to overthrow the British occupation. After gaining many allies—including members of the Muslim Brotherhood, an influential religious group in Egypt—Sadat was content to wait patiently for an opportunity.

For many Egyptians, World War II intensified resentment over British colonialism. Sadat and other officers planned a revolution to rout British forces.

Botched Attempts

The first of several opportunities for action came in the summer of 1941. Sadat and his unit were transferred north to a town called Marsa Matruh on the Mediterranean. His unit was supposed to help the British defend against the advancing forces of Germany's Field Marshal Erwin Rommel. (Rommel was known as the "Desert Fox" because of his clever strategies against the British in the desert.) The British had already suffered defeat at the hands of the Germans in Asia, Europe, and North Africa. Now as the Germans under Rommel moved east across Libya toward Egypt, British authorities began to question the loyalty of the Egyptian troops and ordered them south, out of Marsa Matruh.

Sadat saw this order as his opportunity. He decided that when sent south, he and his unit would wait for the defeat of the British by Rommel. They would then meet with other retreating Egyptian units at some given point and march victoriously together—ahead of the German army—into Cairo.

It was decided that the units would meet at the Mena House, a hotel on a main highway not far from Cairo. Upon arrival, Sadat would, in his own words, "study the plan, make assignments, and choose a suitable time for marching into Cairo to carry out our long-dreamed-of revolution."[16]

When Sadat finally made it to the Mena House, however, he found that his unit was all alone! They waited, but in vain. Later, in his autobiography, Sadat withheld the true reason for the absence of the other units, but it appears the other troops had second thoughts about his plan and purposely backed out. Whatever the reason, the revolution would have to wait, and Sadat later looked upon the dis-

appointment philosophically: "I took it like a sportsman."[17]

This disappointment did not discourage Sadat from his ultimate goal, however. Late in 1941, Sadat became involved in a plan initiated by the Germans. General Azia el-Masri was a former chief of staff in the Egyptian government who had been ousted because of his anti-British views. In late 1941, he was to be secretly flown out of Egypt to Iraq. Once in Baghdad, he was to help in an Iraqi plot to oust the occupying British. Unfortunately, el-Masri's plane crashed a few minutes after takeoff because of a malfunction. While not badly injured, el-Masri was captured by British authorities and taken in for questioning. This was bad news for Sadat, who had helped organize the secret flight. Then a captain in the army, Sadat was taken into custody for his possible connection to the plot.

Sadat was rushed to Cairo for questioning. He expected to be thrown in jail immediately, if only for suspicion of his role in the plot. But when the authorities

Field Marshal Erwin Rommel—also known as the "Desert Fox"—commands German forces in Libya. Although technically British subjects, Sadat and others hoped Rommel would defeat British forces, thereby liberating Egypt from foreign domination.

Hoping to ally his forces with the Germans, Sadat attempted to contact the legendary Desert Fox, pictured here during his North African campaign.

Mediterranean coast. It was clear to Sadat and the other Free Officers that the time to act was near. Sadat had no doubt that Alexandria would soon fall to Rommel, and after that, the Germans would march right into Cairo itself.

Sadat knew that Egyptians did not want to exchange the British yoke for German occupation. Therefore, Sadat planned to ally his movement with the German forces and hope that Germany, in appreciation, would later recognize Egyptian independence.

To this end, Sadat decided it was best to get a message through to Rommel. Sadat and others in the Free Officer's Association would immediately provide maps, including the locations of British installations.

Sadat's first attempt to contact Rommel ended badly. The plane Sadat arranged to carry the message of goodwill to Rommel in El Alamein happened to be a British plane—and it was shot down by the Germans. The pilot, a compatriot of Sadat, was killed, and the message never reached Rommel.

The second attempt to contact Rommel ended in disaster—for Sadat. Sadat had been working with two German spies in Cairo. The spies were caught frolicking on a Nile houseboat by British forces. Among other information, the German spies revealed to the British that Sadat was in communication with them. Consequently, British troops and King Farouk's police woke Sadat in the middle of the night and hustled him away.

After a lengthy attempt to indict Sadat, the Egyptian and British authorities decided to keep him in the Alien's Jail, a penal unit reserved for cases that had any connection to the war. Shortly afterward, he

could produce no evidence against him, he was released a free man. On his way back to his post, he thought about his release and decided he had respect for at least one way the British did things: "That shows, I thought on the way back to the desert, the advantages of the rule of the law."[18]

Contacting Rommel

By the summer of 1942, Rommel had taken the Egyptian town of El Alamein, located only sixty-five miles from the important industrial port city of Alexandria, on the

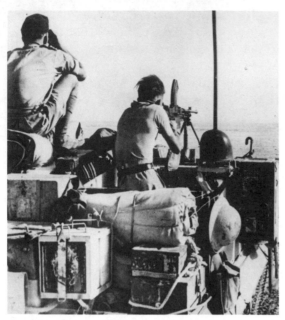

British soldiers during a campaign near El Alamein, where Sadat tried—and failed—to send a message to Rommel.

was transferred to a series of detention centers. He would be in confinement for two years. In that time, Britain would turn the tide of war in its favor and eventually run Rommel out of Egypt.

Alien's Jail

In prison, Sadat underwent a period of introspection and education. He realized that he really wanted little else from life than the liberation of Egypt. If his nation were free, he knew he could be content with a plot of land to farm. Fame, wealth, and renown were really not what he wanted. In jail he spent his time studying books in Arabic and English, and learning German from a fellow prisoner. He also renewed his attachment to his childhood hero, Zahran, martyr to Egyptian liberation from the British.

Unlike his hero Zahran, however, Sadat was able to escape from his captors. In October 1944, he went on a hunger strike and was sent to the new Qasr al-Ayni Hospital. At the hospital he ended his strike and regained his strength. He also made plans for an escape.

One day, during a crowded lunch hour, Sadat made his move. He ran from his guard and outside to the street. A friend, who was a former prisoner, was waiting for him in a small car, with the engine running. Sadat jumped into the car, and they sped off through the busy streets. Sadat was a free man.

Sadat spent the next year as a fugitive, with a new beard and the name Hadji Muhammad. While Sadat went to work in various occupations—including laborer and bus driver—the world watched Britain successfully beat back Rommel's forces. When the war in Europe ended on May 7, 1945, Sadat came out of hiding.

Since wartime regulations no longer applied, officials could not charge him with any offenses. Sadat shaved his beard and sought out his old ally, Gamal Nasser. Together, they vowed to expel the British from Egypt. They were determined to prove that no Egyptian loyal to the British could hide from their wrath.

Execution

Seeking to strike at Egyptian officials loyal to the British, on January 6, 1946, Sadat, Nasser, and other members of the Free Officers carried out the execution of Amin Osman Pasha, the former minister of finance. Pasha had recently made strong pro-British statements to the press and this, Sadat decided, was "tantamount to a self-imposed death sentence."[19]

A young man named Hussein Tewfik was the actual triggerman. Tewfik encountered Pasha as the older man entered a building in downtown Cairo. "Pasha! Pasha!" came the assassin's cries, and Pasha turned around. Tewfik took aim and shot him dead.

Sadat was implicated in the assassination, arrested, and jailed again. Much publicity surrounded his arrest, for the assassination of Pasha was a great psychological blow to the British occupiers. The British now knew that their Egyptian collaborators were not safe among their own people. They also knew that the Egyptian people knew this, too.

The Creation of Israel

Considered a prime catch by the British and their Egyptian collaborators, Sadat this time was sent to Cairo Central Prison. He remained there for eighteen months while going through a long trial over his involvement in the assassination. For much of this time, he was kept in solitary confinement.

But no amount of prison solitude could censor the news that filtered through Cairo Central Prison's walls in 1947: the state of Israel was being re-created. Absent for a thousand years in that part of the world, the state of Israel had gained support since 1917. At that time a British-sponsored resolution, called the Balfour Declaration, recognized the need for a Jewish homeland in the area known

as Palestine. With Jerusalem as its capital, Palestine had been the ancient homeland of the Jews until their military defeat at the hands of the Romans not long after the birth of Jesus Christ.

It wasn't until some thirty years after the Balfour Declaration that the idea of re-creating the state of Israel would take hold. By the end of World War II, in 1945, the nations of the world agreed that a Jewish homeland was necessary. The world had just witnessed the systematic murder of six million European Jews by Nazi Germany.

The Arab nations of the Middle East disagreed with the creation of a Jewish state in their midst. They saw it as a sort of cancer in an otherwise complete and healthy Muslim body. Also, Arabs believed the creation of a Jewish state might displace the Arab populations living in the area known as Palestine. Anwar's friend Nasser would later frame the issue of Israel in these terms: "Israel represents for

us two things: the expulsion of the Palestinian people from their land, and a permanent threat to the Arab nation."[20]

Just hours after the establishment of the state of Israel was proclaimed, the new state was attacked by forces from Jordan, Iraq, Lebanon, Syria, and Egypt. Though the British still occupied Egypt, they did not try to stop the orders of Egypt's King Farouk to attack the newly created neighbor. And though the Egyptian army outnumbered Israeli forces, and had the support of four other Arab armies, the Israelis soundly defeated the total Arab army.

Egyptians all over the country were embarrassed by their role in the Arab defeat. They learned that the king's forces had been poorly trained and poorly led, and their resentment for the regime increased.

Moreover, Egypt and the Arab world greatly resented the treatment of hundreds of thousands of Palestinian Arabs who left Palestine for other Arab countries when Israel was created. Most Palestinian Arabs believed Israel would be wiped out in 1947 by the Arab armies. So they abandoned their homes in Palestine and arrived in neighboring Arab countries, seeking temporary refuge. But after the Arab armies were defeated, the Palestinian Arabs were not integrated into the other Arab societies. Instead they were funneled into rundown and dirty refugee camps, where they were forced to remain until the day Israel would fall.

Those Palestinian Arabs who remained in Palestine during Israel's creation developed their own reasons for resentment. While enjoying better sanitation, medical, and other services than the Palestinians in Arab nations, they came to be treated like second-class citizens in the new Jewish state. The Palestinians were looked upon with distrust in what they felt was their own land. Frustrated and resentful, they, too, waited—and wait still—for liberation.

Jewish youths celebrate in the streets of Israel after the United Nations voted to re-create the Jewish state in Palestine.

Soon after the creation of Israel, Arab troops tried to eradicate their new neighbor. After a crushing defeat, many Arabs were forced to live in refugee camps, such as this one on the Gaza Strip.

Cell 54

While the Arab-Israeli war raged late in 1948, Sadat sat, frustrated, in prison. As the forces of five Arab countries suffered humiliating defeat at the hands of tiny Israel, Sadat longed to be doing his part to aid Egyptian soldiers. "God knows how I suffered at the time! It was agonizing to witness the Israeli air raids on Cairo, violating the sanctity of Ramadan, our holy month. But I was helpless and could do nothing about it."[21]

There was nothing he could do about his living conditions, either. Unlike the Alien's Jail, Cairo Central Prison's living conditions were horrible. "There was no bed, no small table, no chair and no simple lamp. . . . In the winter water oozed from the cell walls day and night, and in the summer huge armies of bugs marched up and down."[22] Sadat was not allowed current books nor a radio. It was difficult to keep up with important events outside the prison walls.

During his eighteen months in Cell 54, Sadat went through another period of self-enlightenment. One aspect of his life that troubled him was his marriage. Back in 1940, at the age of twenty-two, he had married Ekbal Madi, a traditional Muslim woman from his village. Contemplating the marriage from his prison cell, he realized that Ekbal was not the kind of person who could cope with his future. He saw his

Cell 54

In Anwar Sadat, *author Raymond Carroll quotes Sadat's description of the Cairo Central Prison—especially cell number 54:*

"It was four o'clock in the afternoon when I found myself inside Cell 54. I looked around. Cairo Central Prison was completely different from the Alien's Jail. In the first place, there was no bed, no small table, no chair and no simple lamp. It was completely bare—apart from the palm-fibre mat on the macadamized floor, hardly big enough for a man to sleep on, and an unbelievably dirty blanket. You can't imagine how filthy that thing was. In the winter water oozed from the cell walls day and night, and in the summer huge armies of bugs marched up and down. . . . I lived for a whole eighteen months in that hole, unable to read or write or listen to the radio. I was denied everything, even a single lamp."

future as being filled with uncertainty and constant danger. Consequently, he made up his mind to do something about ending the marriage upon his release from prison.

While imprisoned in Cell 54, he thought about other personal issues, too. Through reading the Koran and other books of faith, Sadat discovered the importance of spirituality in his life. One book in particular—*Magnificent Obsession,* by an American, Lloyd Douglas—helped Sadat to learn about faith and love: "This man taught me faith. . . . In Cell 54, I found myself. I found myself and I found that through love I can do miracles. Through hatred I am impotent."[23]

Reading religious books and thinking about love led Sadat to reflect upon his relationship with God. He came to realize that people needed to love God as God loved people. This realization made him happy. Author Raymond Carroll noted that "Immersed in such thoughts, Sadat found his last months in Cairo Central Prison an extremely happy period."[24]

A Free Man

By August 1948, the assassin Tewfik had escaped from prison without ever providing a consistent account of the conspiracy to kill Amin Osman Pasha. Thus, with public opinion strongly supporting him, Sadat was acquitted of aiding the assassination of Pasha and set free. But Sadat became sidetracked from the goals he had set for himself while in prison. He did not immediately divorce his wife, and he became a partner in a business run by his old friend from the army, Hassan Izzat. The partnership turned out badly, however. Sadat did not like constantly haggling over money with Izzat. But a good thing came out of the partnership—he met and fell in love with Izzat's cousin, Jehan. He would marry her the following year, after his divorce from Ekbal.

After having said goodbye to Izzat, Sadat knew the only way he could accomplish his plan for revolution was to rejoin the army. Despite the objection of some pro-British Egyptian officials who distrusted Sa-

dat, an old friend pulled some bureaucratic strings, and Sadat was accepted back into the army as a captain in early 1950.

Back on Track

Sadat quickly hooked up with his old friend Nasser in their secret organization within the Egyptian army, the Free

In the early 1950s, Egyptians were eager for change. In Cairo, throngs of protesters carry large placards denouncing the British.

Officer's Association. As before, the goal of the organization was clear and simple: revolution. Other Arab countries had already begun to throw off the yoke of their British bosses, and the Free Officers took this as encouragement.

Since Sadat's absence, the organization had grown. Nasser was firmly at the head. Nasser alerted his old friend that the best thing he could do was to ask for an army promotion in order to be in control of as much information as possible. Sadat applied for his promotion and it was granted immediately. The position was better than imagined: Sadat was to be a spy, reporting on the activities of rebel organizations—like the Free Officer's Association! He could now play the role of double agent, and his aid to the association would be invaluable.

The conditions in Egypt in the early 1950s were ripe for revolution. Besides the embarrassment over King Farouk's failure to halt the creation of the state of Israel, Farouk's inability to handle Egypt's social and economic problems stoked the anger of most Egyptians. About 95 percent of all Egyptians suffered from poverty and joblessness, while a small class of influential people close to the king prospered. Strikes and demonstrations of disapproval were rampant.

Other revolutionary groups in Egypt, such as the Moslem Brotherhood, were also pressuring the government. In fact, when a friendship treaty was signed between the British and the Egyptians before the war was terminated in 1950, freedom fighters and members of the Muslim Brotherhood began harassing the British at their military base in the Suez Canal Zone. The Brotherhood was letting the British know they were not welcome there,

and their presence would not be tolerated without a struggle.

The Free Officers set the date for revolution in November 1952. But events were happening rapidly. In the early summer of 1952, the leaders of the association discovered that King Farouk was in fact planning a counterattack against them. Nasser realized they would have to strike out at the king immediately.

On July 21, Nasser summoned Sadat to Cairo with the message that the revolution was imminent. Sadat arrived in Cairo, expecting to be met by representatives of his organization, but no one was there. Thinking he had arrived ahead of sched-

King Farouk's failure to stop the creation of Israel and handle Egypt's domestic ills sapped his popular support and heralded the end of the monarchy.

"The Heroic Image of My Dreams"

In her book, A Woman of Egypt, *Jehan Sadat remembers her response to the practical advice given by her brother—stay away from the older, ex-prisoner Anwar Sadat:*

"But what fifteen-year-old girl is practical? I looked at his skin, much darker than mine and in the opinion of many Egyptians less appealing, and found him very handsome. I looked at his one rumpled white jacket and one pair of trousers, and found him flawlessly dressed. I looked at the age on his face, fifteen years more than mine, and saw the ideals of youth. I listened to his silence and heard a strong personality I could admire. He was the heroic image of my dreams."

ule, he went home by himself and spent the evening with Jehan at one of Cairo's open-air movie theaters. They sat together through three featured movies.

While Sadat watched movies, Nasser seized power. The Free Officers stormed the government's Army Command Headquarters in Cairo, and Farouk's chief of staff was put under house arrest. Meanwhile, the Free Officers unit commanders were poised on the outskirts of Cairo, waiting for orders to march into the city with troops and tanks.

Upon returning home at 12:45 in the morning, Sadat discovered urgent messages left for him by Nasser. He understood, then, that the revolution was underway. Sadat mentioned none of this to his wife. He merely got into his uniform,

strapped on his pistol, and hurried out into the dark.

The takeover was accomplished with little bloodshed. The Free Officer's Association had announced their demands, and the authorities, knowing they had no power left, quickly and quietly accepted their fate. British troops were no problem—they were wisely ordered by their superiors to stay in their barracks.

Sadat himself was assigned by Nasser to announce the news to the world from the Broadcasting House in Cairo. The streets were filled with happy, dancing Egyptians, celebrating the new leadership of Gamal Abdel Nasser. Three days later, King Farouk, allowed to board the royal yacht, sailed away from his country forever.

3 In Nasser's Shadow

The new leadership, with Nasser as its commander, was quick to establish its authority. The Constituent Council, which had been the ruling body of the revolutionary officers, was now named the Revolutionary Command Council (RCC). Nasser became its chairman and leader. The RCC was made up of Nasser's close allies—including Sadat—appointed to administrate various sectors of the government. Seeing the need for continuity, Nasser also gave council positions to some of King Farouk's top officials.

In the first months of Nasser's rule, there were signs of power struggles within the council. Many of the council members were fighting each other for power and scrambling for positions of control and influence.

Sadat was outraged over the infighting. He expected more cooperation from the men of the new regime than the behavior of the old regime. As author Raymond Carroll reported, "In Sadat's mind, the heads of these supposed revolutionary leaders had been turned by power. . . .

After routing the old regime, the Revolutionary Command Council meets in Cairo. As the driving force behind the revolution, Gamal Abdel Nasser became leader and chairman of the council.

They went so far as to divide the country into personal 'spheres of influence,' within which they could turn a profit for themselves and produce rewards for their followers and friends."[25]

Sadat thought Nasser should rule with a more authoritative hand. In fact, he thought Nasser should be more of a dictator than a democratically oriented leader. Sadat felt that only a leader with absolute powers could ensure quick and necessary changes in a country with internal struggles, worker strikes, and security threats that could threaten the regime.

Sadat's fears for the security of the new regime were realized in late 1952. A major plot devised by politicians from the Farouk era and some army officers was

Nasser on his way to the Revolutionary Command Council headquarters as he takes over the government of Egypt.

discovered. By January 1952, Nasser, acting quickly and decisively, put an end to the plot.

With this experience behind him, Nasser saw the need to take measures to protect the new government. In the early months of 1953 he confiscated all the property of the royal family. Nasser thought they might use their money to organize resistance against him. The royal family's money and property, amounting to millions of dollars, went to rural health centers, schools, and hospitals. Nasser also promoted his friend Abdel Hakim Amer to commander in chief of the armed forces. Nasser also gave himself the posts of deputy premier and interior minister. The Revolutionary Command Council announced that it would assume all legislative and executive powers in the country for the next three years. Finally, the fanatical Moslem Brotherhood, a revolutionary religious group in favor of turning Egypt over to religious rule, was now banned from all activity in Egypt.

Egypt Under Nasser

With a firmer grip on the country, Nasser felt free to move ahead with his goals. He wanted to strengthen Egypt's feeble economy, so he created government industries to help expand the economy. Health plans and new schools were developed. And eventually, individual income began rising for all Egyptians.

In late 1952 and early 1953, land reforms were put into effect. The land reforms changed the amount of land each Egyptian could own. Under King Farouk, each man could have an unlimited

amount of land. Under Nasser's new Agrarian Reform Law, two hundred acres was the most anyone could own. Men with more than two hundred acres had their holdings reduced. Poor, landless farmers, on the other hand, were granted free parcels of land. Perhaps the most important outcome of the Agrarian Land Reform was the pride and sense of participation it gave to those who had felt cut off from the land since the rule of Farouk.

Nasser also announced his plans for building the Aswan High Dam at the city of Aswan in Upper Egypt. The dam would control the waters of the Nile River, which had risen and fallen throughout Egyptian history. Work on a hydroelectric station at

Under Nasser's leadership, Egypt began to rebuild itself. This included the development of new schools, such as this one in Alexandria.

In an attempt to spur economic growth, Nasser planned the construction of the Aswan High Dam at the ancient Egyptian town Aswan. Western nations offered—and later withdrew—financial support for this massive project.

Aswan began in 1953. The electricity from this station was essential to the building of the dam, which would begin in the 1960s. In 1956 several Western nations and international banks agreed to help finance the project. Nasser accepted their offers with enthusiasm and gratitude.

Finally, the new regime worked diligently to evict the British from Egypt. Britain signed the Anglo-Egyptian Evacuation Agreement on October 19, 1954. Twenty months later, the British presence—strong for seventy-five years—was gone.

An Accord with the Soviets

Having made significant economic reforms, the new government was determined to become a strong military power. To this end, Nasser asked the United States to supply Egypt with weapons. At the time, the United States was entrenched in the cold war with the Soviet Union. Both superpowers were seeking alliances and strategic positions in the Middle East.

The U.S. response to Egypt's request for arms was disappointing. The United States told Egypt they could have weapons if they signed a pact stating they would be an ally of the United States and would never use the arms against them. Furthermore, American arms experts would have to come along with the weapons to Egypt, thus creating a small but significant American strategic presence in the country.

Nasser was displeased. He and the Egyptian people felt strongly about maintaining Egypt's independence. He did not want any strings attached to Egypt's inter-

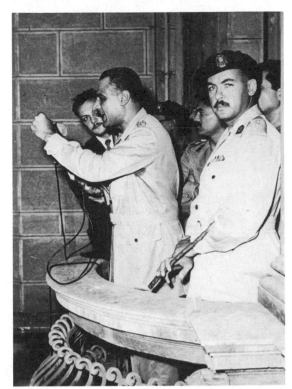

Nasser addresses a jubilant crowd after the signing of the Anglo-Egyptian Evacuation Agreement, which ended seventy-five years of British occupation.

national dealings. When the United States offered the weapons for free, Nasser refused, because of conditions the United States would impose. The United States offered deal after deal, but Nasser refused each one because he felt Egyptian independence would be compromised. He grew resentful and bitter toward the United States.

Egypt went without a central weapons supplier for several years. Then in 1955, Nasser, desperate for a deal, signed an agreement with Soviet leader Nikita Khrushchev. At the time, Nasser was glad to cement relations with a world power. In time, though, Nasser would regret ever having chosen to do business with the So-

Nasser toasts Soviet leader Nikita Khrushchev, who, in 1955, agreed to supply weapons to Egypt.

viets. Among the problems, the Soviets delayed arms shipments and sent Egypt outdated equipment. As Sadat later recalled, the Soviet treatment of Nasser was "neither generous nor dignified."[26]

Sadat in the Shadows

While Nasser ruled as Egypt's visible figurehead, Sadat was content to stay in the shadows and do the bidding of the president. In his post as head of Nasser's Islamic Congress, Sadat traveled to other Muslim countries for purposes of friendship and diplomacy. Sadat was so passively compliant to Nasser's orders that Nasser began

to kiddingly refer to him as "Major Yes Yes." Nasser even complained that if only Sadat would vary his continual "sah," or "Yes, Sir," Sadat's servility would be easier to bear!

Despite this ribbing, Nasser knew Sadat was a trusted and reliable ally. And Sadat would later say, "From my record in the armed forces, and from his experience since we first met early in life, [Nasser] gathered I was a man of principles and lofty values. It wasn't difficult for Nasser to realize that he could rely on me."[27]

Of course, Sadat did other things besides saying "Yes, Sir" all the time. He became the editor in chief of *Gomhouriyeh* (Arabic for "The Republic"), the newspaper created by the RCC. Sadat also wrote articles which supported the government and its policies.

One issue Sadat heatedly wrote about was the Baghdad Pact, proposed by British prime minister Anthony Eden. Eden insisted that Britain's departure from Egypt had created a power vacuum. In order to keep the Soviets from filling this vacuum, nations in the area had to vow to work together to keep the Soviets out.

While Iraq, Pakistan, and Turkey, fearing Soviet influence, were quick to sign the Baghdad Pact, Egypt refused. Sadat said recent events in Egypt were reason enough to avoid signing the pact. "Having just put an end to British occupation in October 1954 we could hardly be expected to tie Egypt down to a British-controlled pact or to any other foreign power."[28] While Sadat won praise from other Arab nations, such as Jordan and Lebanon, who agreed not to sign the pact, he received contempt from the British and their allies, including the United States.

While Arab nations talked of unity,

Sadat was a trusted ally of Nasser. Sadat said of their close friendship that "it wasn't difficult for Nasser to realize that he could rely on me."

Wildly cheering crowds greet Nasser after his decision to nationalize the Suez Canal.

Nasser's cabinet became anything but unified. Despite the purge of 1953, plenty of leaders in the government still vied for prestige and power. Nasser had grown distrustful of many around him. Sadat understood Nasser's growing suspicions and was relieved when Nasser again took action.

After being elected president again in June 1956 in a plebiscite (a direct vote by an entire people), Nasser disbanded the RCC. When asked to serve in Nasser's new government, Sadat politely declined. He told Nasser he would serve as a consultant or advisor, and that Nasser could always depend on him for that. But he had seen enough corruption in government to want to remain on the outside of it. Author Raymond Carroll wrote that "In Sa-

dat's opinion, hate dominated the ruling group, and he wanted to keep his distance from it." [29]

Nationalizing the Canal

In the summer of 1956, Nasser made a move with which Sadat strongly disagreed: Nasser nationalized the Suez Canal. This meant the canal would be owned by the government instead of being privately owned.

Built in the nineteenth century, the Suez Canal is a wide channel cut into the earth at the western border of the Sinai Peninsula. The canal provides passage between the Red Sea and the Mediterranean Sea. It also provided revenues for Britain and France, its joint owners who were responsible for its construction a hundred years before.

Sadat felt that an armed response by the British and French would occur in the wake of nationalization. Sadat also believed that Egyptian troops were not ready for such a confrontation. Despite his concern, Sadat was proud of Nasser's move. According to author Raymond Carroll, "To the vast majority of Egyptians, after seventy-five years of humiliating subservience to the British, his countrymen were ready to idolize the man who dared to tweak the tail of the British lion."[30]

Nasser's reasons for claiming the canal were clear enough. He was retaliating against the United States for cancelling

In June 1956, Nasser announces that Egypt has nationalized the Suez Canal in order to use its revenues to build the Aswan High Dam.

loans for the Aswan High Dam project. The United States cancelled the loans when Nasser purchased arms from Czechoslovakia and officially recognized Communist China. These two acts were at odds with the political positions of the United States. Nasser believed the canal's revenues could be used to finance the Aswan High Dam project. The revenues primarily came from fees ships paid for passing through the canal from the Mediterranean Sea to the Red Sea.

Nasser also wanted to show Egyptians, as well as the rest of the world, that Egypt was a strong and independent nation and naturally held claim to everything within its borders.

But Nasser's show of strength also threatened Egypt's neighbors. By attempting to protect and maintain their own waters, Egypt's navy sealed off the Straits of Tiran. The straits, located in the Red Sea just off the southeast coast of the Sinai Peninsula, were the only passageway to Israel's southern port city Eilat. Consequently, Eilat was also sealed off from its important shipping routes. International tensions escalated quickly. To Israel, Egypt's act was an act of war. On October 29, 1956, Israeli ground troops backed by the British and French air forces confronted Egyptian forces.

Anwar Sadat learned at least one important lesson about allies from the 1956 war. During the height of battle, Shukri al-Kuwatli, president of Syria, was in Moscow. He asked the Soviet leadership if they could quickly supply Egypt with arms. Moscow flatly refused. Sadat would later say, "this made me believe, from that moment on, that it was always futile to depend on the Soviet Union."[31]

The Israeli-European alliance methodically battered the Egyptian army, capturing the Gaza Strip and all of Egypt's Sinai Peninsula. Egypt had clearly taken a bad beating. Though the battle had been lost, the war continued—in diplomatic circles. U.S. president Eisenhower feared the Soviets would become involved and support Egypt. Wishing to avoid this kind of superpower confrontation, Eisenhower urged Britain and France to withdraw from the area.

The Soviet Union also warned the two countries to retreat from Egypt. This warning, however, was issued after Britain and France had already responded to Eisenhower's warning! It was obviously a bit of muscle-flexing for the Soviets. In any event, by March 1957, Israel, under pressure from the United States, also pulled back, and Egypt once again had control of its land—including the Suez Canal.

Nasser's popularity in Egypt and throughout the Arab world escalated tremendously because of the battle. He had fought the West, and even in military defeat, Egypt had won at the diplomatic table: the Suez Canal would remain under their control. Arab nations were buoyed by Nasser's achievement. Talk of Arab unity began to spread throughout the nations of the Middle East.

Of course, Sadat was pleased with the outcome of the war. But he would later state that he thought Nasser had not learned the right lessons from the experience. In Sadat's opinion, Nasser should have made an effort to form a friendship with the United States instead of praising the actions—or nonactions—of the Soviet Union. Sadat later said:

Following Nasser's claim to the Suez Canal, relations with Britain, France, and Israel deteriorated. On October 29, 1956, these three countries launched an invasion of Egypt. This photo shows a sunken British ship at the entrance of the canal.

Israeli tanks advance toward the Suez Canal in November 1956. Soon after, the Israeli government agreed to withdraw its forces from the captured territory.

He attributed the failure of the 1956 tripartite aggression to the Russian 'warning,' and praised the role of the Soviet Union in complete disregard of Eisenhower's efforts and his direct orders to Britain and France to withdraw from Egypt.[32]

Back to Work

After the 1956 war, Sadat went back to work in Nasser's shadow. In 1957, he published *Revolt on the Nile*, a book in which he wove together historical analysis with his personal memoirs. In this book and a soon-to-follow portrait of his boss titled *My Son, This Is Your Uncle Gamal*, he confirmed his deep feeling and commitment to Nasser. In his book *Sadat and His Statecraft*, author Felipe Fernandez-Armesto wrote:

> Sadat was never hesitant in hero-worship or temperate in enthusiasm. . . . While Nasser lived, he [Sadat] was enthralled by him and responded wholeheartedly to the leader's allure. Only later could Sadat reconsider the relationship in something like detachment.[33]

Besides writing for Nasser, Sadat took on other government responsibilities and often spoke for his boss. After the 1956 war, Sadat was appointed secretary general of the new 200-member Constituent Assembly. In this post, he organized discus-

In February 1958, Nasser addresses a huge crowd after becoming the first president of the United Arab Republic.

sions among the members in an attempt to define the purposes, policies, and goals of the revolution.

In 1958, after Syria, Egypt, and, later, Yemen, united to form the United Arab Republic (which fell apart three years later), Sadat became speaker of the Joint Parliament, which represented the Republic. Sadat further sharpened his speaking abilities in 1959, when he spoke out against Egypt's former ally, the Soviet Union. Soviet leader Nikita Khrushchev had voiced his disapproval of the non-Communist alliance of Egypt, Syria, and Yemen. A few years later, in 1961, Sadat engaged in a shouting match with the Soviet premier after Khrushchev condemned Nasser and his regime for persecuting Egyptian Communists.

Well aware of Egypt's coolness towards the Soviet Union, the United States, at this time, privately offered Nasser any supplies and goods he might need. But Nasser did not want to become indebted to the United States and proclaimed that Egypt would only accept wheat and petroleum—goods which helped Egypt immensely. Sadat, looking on, disagreed with Nasser's hard line. Sadat thought Egypt could have benefitted greatly by responding more favorably to the United States.

The year 1959 dealt Sadat a hard blow. His mother, Sit el-Barrein, died. He had a tomb built for her in the village of his birth, Mit Abul-Kum. He was despondent for days and found it difficult to hide his sorrow.

Around this time he became reinterested in the village of his birth. In a few years, he would buy a seventeen-acre plot of land near the village and build a house on it. Sadat's political identity would be strongly tied to his roots in village life. Sadat viewed himself as a rural man at heart.

It was not long before Sadat was politically active again. Expanding upon his duties as secretary general of the Constituent Assembly, Sadat began to play the role of warmonger. Throughout the sixties, one of his most frequent targets, in print or from a podium, was Israel. The humiliations of 1948 and 1956 provided fuel for revenge among all Egyptians. As the years passed, the talk of attacking Israel steadily increased in Egypt—and throughout the Arab world as well.

The Six Day War

By the spring of 1967, the Arab world was prepared to try to destroy tiny Israel once again. On May 22, as it had done eleven years earlier, Egypt's navy closed the Straits of Tiran, thus cutting off shipping

Field Marshal Abdel Hakim Amer gives a pep talk to Egyptian forces amassed along the Egyptian-Israeli border.

to Israel's southern port city of Eilat. Egypt cast out U.N. peacekeeping forces stationed in the Sinai Peninsula and began a massive troop buildup. Syria and Jordan also massed troops along their borders with Israel. In June 1967, the Six Day War erupted.

On June 5, as the first shots were being fired, Field Marshal Abdel Hakim Amer, lifelong friend of Nasser and an important figure in the July 1952 revolution, flew off for a quick tour of Egyptian troops in the Sinai. Naturally, gunfire on the Egyptian side was halted so as not to endanger Amer's flight. In this momentary lapse of fire, Israel attacked. Planes from secret bases flew north over the Mediterranean and banked south over Egypt. Sixteen Egyptian airfields and most of the aircraft on them were destroyed. By midmorning "almost four hundred Egyptian aircraft had been put out of commission."[34] Similar Israeli attacks devastated Syrian and Jordanian positions. The war was virtually decided in the first few hours of battle.

In the Wake of Defeat

For Egypt, the war was a disgrace. Leading up to the war, Nasser had raised expectations in the Arab world by taunting Israel and assuring them that the Israelis would be driven into the sea.

But, in fact, Egyptian forces were not fully prepared. Part of the blame for this fell on the shoulders of Amer. It was later determined that Abdel Hakim Amer misled a number of government officials about the readiness of the Egyptian armed forces.

Egypt was forced to face the reality of the situation. They had lost the war. They

(Above) An Israeli convoy moves toward the Sinai Desert after the Six Day War erupted. (Below) Against a backdrop of flames and barbed wire, an Egyptian goes through "commando" training as part of the Egyptian military buildup in 1967.

had been soundly defeated in less than six days. Not only had they lost the battle, but Israel now controlled the entire Sinai Peninsula, which had served as a sort of buffer zone for Egypt. Plus, the Israelis were practically a stone's throw from the Suez Canal and the Egyptian mainland. To create a formidable line of defense, the Israelis constructed the Bar-Lev Line, a series of earth and concrete bunkers on the eastern bank of the Suez Canal. Meanwhile, the Egyptians, according to author George Sullivan, "agonized over their defeat."[35]

Sadat was deeply disturbed by the defeat. Sullivan wrote that "Sadat described himself as being overwhelmed" by it.[36] He cut off his outside contacts with the world for a few weeks after the war so he would not have to hear criticisms of Egypt and its armed forces.

When finished grieving, however, he

was determined to find out what had gone wrong. He conducted an investigation and found what he had suspected was the reason behind the poor performance of Egyptian troops: a lack of strong and competent leadership. Sadat found that during the few days of battle, there was much confusion among the Egyptian troops. The confusion was due to a lack of preparation by their officers, chief among them Field Marshal Amer. The lack of preparation was rooted in a centuries-old lack of leadership, which was due to Egypt's domination by colonial powers.

According to author Felipe Fernandez-Armesto, Sadat would learn several lessons from the war. One was that Nasser himself should have taken visible command over the war instead of leaving it to unreliable

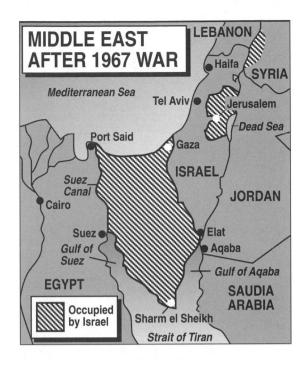

Captured Egyptian soldiers—their uniforms marked and their feet bare—march in a prisoner-of-war camp where they are held by the Israelis.

Yasser Arafat (left), Nasser (center), and King Hussein (right) at a meeting of the Arab Summit Conference in September 1970. Nasser died shortly afterward of a heart attack.

men like Amer. Sadat believed that this would have increased morale as Nasser was a popular man.

Secondly, Sadat realized that the war on Israel was very popular with Egyptians. Perhaps it was this realization that made him feel positive about the War of Attrition with Israel that began the following year, in September 1968. In this war, Egypt began a series of strikes on Israeli forces in the Sinai. Their intent was to wear down Israel's resistance and staying power.

Nasser did not take defeat as constructively as Sadat. Humiliated and defeated, he resigned. But the masses, expressing their admiration and empathy for him, rallied and demanded he remain their

leader. So Nasser continued on, depressed over Egypt's failure and his own worsening physical condition. He had been suffering for years from diabetes, heart trouble, and an unidentifiable illness that caused him enormous pain in his legs.

In December 1969, Nasser approached Sadat and asked him to be vice president. Sadat's response was to politely decline. But Nasser was firm. The leader had suffered a heart attack in September and knew that his time was running out. He knew he had to name a successor to avoid a damaging power struggle in the wake of his own demise. Sadat then accepted his leader's request.

In 1970, Nasser concentrated on improving Egypt's military. Far-reaching changes were made. Leaders were kicked out, such as Nasser's friend Field Marshal Amer, who, in disgrace, committed suicide. Illiterate soldiers were replaced by high school and college graduates. Higher pay was granted. The Egyptian army had a new face, and it tested itself by making periodic raids into the Sinai and attacking Israeli installations in the War of Attrition. This series of conflicts would last for several years.

While Nasser had success with changing the army, he continued to have problems with his main allies, the Soviets. Soviet advisors—between twelve and fifteen thousand of them—were sprinkled throughout the Egyptian forces, assigned to every military unit. Egypt therefore felt it was not in complete control of its fighting forces. Also, Moscow kept promising weapons but never delivered them on time. Plus, Nasser had already broken relationships with the United States and other Western powers in order to please the Soviets, a fact that was never lost on Sadat.

According to author George Sullivan, "it became obvious to Sadat that Nasser had painted himself into a corner."[37]

End of an Era

Despite Nasser's shortcomings, no one doubted his tremendous contributions to Egypt. In the years of Nasser's leadership, Egypt had undergone tremendous change. Under Nasser, land cultivation increased 15 percent and kept up with the growing population, which went from twenty million to forty million between the years 1952 and 1978. The number of students, both male and female, in schools and institutions of higher learning increased an incredible 300 percent. From one doctor for every five thousand people in 1953, the number went to one doctor per every two thousand. The average life expectancy rose from forty-three to fifty-two.

As 1970 wore on, Nasser's health declined. At a meeting of the Arab Summit

An Uncomfortable Moment

In his book, Autumn of Fury, *Mohamed Heikal recalls that Egyptian officials looked forward to supporting Sadat but were upset by a simple physical gesture:*

"After he had been duly elected, Sadat appeared before Parliament and pledged himself to carry on along the path Nasser had charted. 'My programme is Nasser's,' he said. But when he had finished speaking he made the mistake of bowing to a bust of Nasser which stood in the chamber. There was a murmur of disapproval; such a gesture smacked of idolatry."

Mourners reach out to touch the flag-draped coffin of Gamal Abdel Nasser, whose vision and leadership made him a symbol of Arab nationalism.

Conference in Cairo in September, Nasser appeared exhausted. Suddenly on September 28, 1970, Sadat was summoned to Nasser's home. As George Sullivan wrote:

> When he arrived, he was shown into Nasser's bedroom. What he saw made him gasp. The Egyptian leader was in bed surrounded by doctors, the bedcover over his face. The doctors told Sadat that Nasser had died of a heart attack about an hour before.
>
> Sadat lifted the bedcover. Nasser looked as though he might only be asleep. "I put my cheek against his but did not feel the chill of death," Sadat says in his book. He turned to the doctors and said, "It's not true. What you're saying is wrong. It can't be right!"
>
> The doctors assured Sadat that they had done all they could possibly do. Sadat burst into tears.[38]

Nasser's funeral took place three days later. Leaders from throughout the world came to pay their respects. Millions thronged the streets of Cairo, lamenting the passing of their leader. Sadat's daughter Camelia remembers, "People could be seen wandering in the streets crying Nasser's name. 'Good-bye, Nasser,' they wailed. 'Good-bye, our leader!'"[39]

With the president dead, Anwar Sadat, the country's only vice president, became acting president of Egypt.

4 The New Leader

Nine days after the death of Gamal Abdel Nasser, 353 members of the Egyptian National Assembly elected Sadat as the new leader of the country. This did not mean, though, that they had complete confidence in his ability to rule. Rather, many of them thought he would be a weak leader, one who could be easily manipulated. At this point in time, in author Fernandez-

Egypt's National Assembly elected Sadat president nine days after Nasser's death.

Armesto's words, "it was impossible to prophesy the greatness of Sadat's future role. He always skirted the center of the stage, he always shunned the place of a leader."[40]

Sadat, though, was not ignorant of the assembly members' motivations. He found out the ruling Supreme Executive Committee of the Arab Socialist Union, Nasser's political party, was planning a conspiracy against him. Sadat's rivals in the party wanted to postpone a public vote that would approve Sadat's presidency. By postponing the vote, the rival party could weaken Sadat's authority, and one of their own might ultimately rise to the presidency.

Acting quickly, Sadat ordered the public to vote immediately. On October 15, 1970, less than three weeks after the death of Nasser, the country overwhelmingly approved his selection. He was sworn into office for a six-year term. With the failure of their plan, Sadat's enemies in the government plotted their next move against him.

The New Leader

Egyptians approved of Sadat as their leader mainly because they believed he would provide continuity of leadership. He was, after all, the legitimate successor to Nasser and thus the obvious choice for the job. Sadat was left with a nation with many problems, however. Egypt faced a housing shortage in Cairo, loss of income from the abandoned Suez Canal and the Sinai oilfields, due to the 1967 war with Israel, and a difficult and often unreliable relationship with Moscow.

Sadat realized he now had the power to put his ideals into action and make the changes that would help his country:

> Now that I was President, I felt I wielded a tremendous *real* power, which had to be used in doing good. . . . Never had I had a better chance of putting my principles into practice than when the people elected me President.[41]

Besides what his newfound power enabled him to do, Sadat seemed to enjoy his power for its own sake. Journalist Mohamed Heikal wrote that "his new honorific position gave Sadat such obvious pleasure."[42]

Doubts

Though he had gained the Egyptian peoples' vote of confidence, Sadat had difficulty gaining the confidence of foreign leaders. They thought of him as a transitional figure, who would be replaced after a short stay in office. Richard Nixon, then president of the United States, sent cabinet member Elliott Richardson as a special representative to Egypt to express American condolences about Nasser's death. After meeting with Sadat, Richardson wrote that he was sure the new leader would last no longer than eight weeks.

Fellow leaders in the Egyptian government privately scorned Sadat for not being an independent figure. Some called him "Nasser's poodle."[43] The Egyptian people doubted Sadat. They made fun of Sadat's rise to power. Most residents of Cairo did not even recognize his photograph when it appeared on posters plastered throughout the city. And certain seg-

U.S. cabinet member Elliott Richardson talks to the newly elected Sadat following Nasser's funeral. Richardson believed that Sadat's term in office would be short-lived.

ments of Egyptian society that did recognize him scorned him for his dark skin and peasant background.

First Steps

On his first day of office, Anwar Sadat showed that his rule would be unique and that he would not be content to be a mere copy of Gamal Nasser. When some of his staff brought in a pile of tapes of telephone conversations of suspected foes of the government, Sadat ordered them burned. He thereby ended the policy of spying, begun by Nasser.

Sadat made radical decisions soon after taking office. In Nasser's day, prominent private citizens who had different political beliefs from the government could be considered enemies of the people. As a result, their land could be taken over by the government. In December 1970, Sadat officially put an end to this policy. By doing away with this arbitrary seizure of land, Sadat won acclaim from Egyptians all over the country. Of course, officials who had benefitted from the seizures reacted with hostility toward Sadat. Some of them were forced to give back the lands they had already seized.

Another important early step was ending the War of Attrition with Israel. Many of Sadat's advisors encouraged him to continue striking Israeli targets in the Sinai to bruise the morale of the Israeli forces. Sadat, however, feared the conflict would become a full-fledged war. He decided that Egyptian forces, still suffering from the 1967 disaster, were not yet ready for an all-out fight with Israel once again.

In the meantime, Sadat hoped to win

In a dramatic move to liberalize Nasser's authoritarian regime, Sadat throws documents containing details of bugged telephone conversations into a fire.

back the Sinai by negotiation. In February 1971, he offered his "Initiative for Peace." The initiative offered to stop the strikes on Israeli targets if Israeli forces withdrew from Egyptian land. The Egyptian people greeted the proposal with pride and enthusiasm. The Israelis, however, questioned the language of the document. They also doubted whether any Arab leader would actually stand behind his words. Thus they refused the proposal. In the eyes of the world, however, Sadat came out looking good. He had asked for peace, and Israel had rejected it.

Though Sadat looked good on the world stage, at home his leadership was in danger. While in Moscow in March 1971,

Sadat with his wife Jehan. Through Jehan, Sadat learned of an assassination plot against him.

Sadat had reprimanded the Soviets for stalling during the Nasser years. He also refused to accept Moscow's various conditions for Egypt's use of Soviet arms.

Back in Cairo, Sadat found that his pro-Marxist colleagues in the Egyptian government were seething with anger over his defiant stance toward Moscow. He soon confirmed that a conspiracy did indeed exist against him. It was being orchestrated by the Soviet-aligned Ali Sabri. A former Nasser cabinet official and now one of Sadat's vice presidents, Sabri was working with other government insiders to freeze Sadat out of the government.

The plot thickened during a meeting of the Higher Executive Committee of the Socialist Union on April 21. Sadat called for the committee to vote on approving a union between Egypt, Syria, and Libya. Discussions between the three countries regarding unity and cooperation had been going on for several years. Syrian and Libyan leaders basically agreed with Sadat's support for the merger, but they told Sadat, in confidence, that they had gotten negative messages about the proposed union from other Egyptian government officials. Those officials included Ali Sabri and Minister of the Interior Sharawi Gomaa.

Now it was Egypt's turn to decide on the merger. If approved, the new union would require new elections for officials of the new governing institutions that would be created to administer the joint effort. The change would give Sadat the chance to get his opponents out of power. If the Egyptian vote approved the union, the vote would also show support for Sadat. When only three out of four hundred members raised their hands in support of the union, Sadat knew he had to act quickly or be forced out of the government.

Then Sadat learned of an even more diabolical plot against him. Members of the cabinet secretly approached Sadat's wife Jehan and told her to warn her husband of an assassination plot against him. When Sadat first learned of the plot, he pretended to ignore it. His wife was upset with his calmness. When she exclaimed that other high-level officials—the minister of defense, the minister of information, and the minister of the interior— were not with him, he merely responded, "Don't worry. God is with us."[44]

Sadat learned that plotters planned to assassinate him while he traveled to the coast city of Alexandria. He cancelled the trip. That night, May 11, was a tense one. Sadat kept his pistol loaded by his bedside with the door locked. He asked his daughter Loubna to sleep at a friend's house. Loubna refused, saying she wanted to stick by her father. Sadat's fifteen-year-old son also remained in the house, standing guard with a hunting rifle. The arrival of soldiers later in the night eased everyone's mind, and the night passed without incident.

The next day, Sadat acted against the plotters. He jailed his chief adversary, Ali Sabri, and accused him of tapping the presidential telephone. Others faithful to Sabri were jailed and accused of corruption, embezzlement, and bribery. Three days later, Sharawi Gomaa was accused of being the leader of the plotters and was dismissed from the government. Other cabinet members handed in their resignations. They believed their departure would paralyze Sadat's government and lead to its downfall. But Sadat replaced the old guard with men of his own, and his power remained intact.

Sadat took advantage of the situation to gain the support of the Egyptian people. Appealing to the public's compassion, he told the story of the Ali Sabri conspiracy. Author Raymond Carroll wrote that one of Sadat's strengths as a ruler was his "intuitive grasp of what the people wanted."[45]

What did Sadat's victory over his political rivals show the world? Scholar Raymond A. Hinnebusch Jr. believes the message was twofold. To Moscow, it gave the message that Egyptian leaders who had been sympathetic to the Soviets were out of office. To the West, it said Egypt was no longer a client state of the Soviet Union and was therefore willing to be more open to advice and advances.[46]

The world may not have seen, however, how much help Sadat received in thwarting his conspirators. As would happen several times throughout his career, Sadat would be assisted—even rescued—

On May 15, 1971, a televised Sadat tells his countrymen that the attempted coup against him was nothing more than a "storm in a teacup."

"Grind, Sadat, Grind!"

After Sadat foiled the May 1971 attempted coup against him, the Egyptian people celebrated. In her book, A Woman of Egypt, *Jehan Sadat recalls the day after the coup's failure:*

"From such a night of tension came a morning of rejoicing. As Anwar spoke from his heart over radio and television, people began to pour into the streets. 'Any force against my country, any threat to the new liberty and freedom I am giving to you all, I will grind into mincemeat,' he promised with great emotion. The people went mad with joy, picking up on the phrase that had come to identify my husband during what would be called the Corrective Revolution. 'Ufrum, Sadat, ufrum!' they chanted in the streets, massing in front of our house. 'Grind, Sadat, grind!' Soon we could see handpainted posters among the crowd, cartoons of the various ministers falling into meat grinders and coming out as mincemeat. 'We are behind you, Sadat,' the mobs called. 'We are with you!'"

by those faithful to either him or the principles of government. In the conspiracy, General Sadiq, chief of staff of the Egyptian army, was called to a meeting with General Fawzi, minister of war. Fawzi asked Sadiq if he "was ready" to overthrow the leader. But Sadiq refused and accused Fawzi of dragging the army into politics, a place it did not belong. "If you want to resign, you can," said Sadiq, "but the army is not going to move. It's all over." The other senior officers present at the meeting sided with Sadiq. Mohamed Heikal, editor of the Cairo daily newspaper *Al Ahram* and friend to both Nasser and Sadat, wrote:

So the coup failed. But although Sadat emerged the hero of the hour, who had almost single-handedly routed the formidable phalanx of his enemies, he

had not had to do anything at all. He had been rescued by luck, and by the discipline of the army.[47]

Sadat was soon supported by the majority of Egyptians. Much of his popularity came from the policies he initiated. These policies gave Egyptians a sense of openness about their society. In May 1971 he declared, echoing the first days of his rule, that any secret tapes still held by the minister of the interior's office would be burned. Also, detention centers for political prisoners were to be shut down. Arbitrary arrests were put to an end, and open criticism of the government was officially allowed. Anwar Sadat continued efforts to show his people and the world that his regime would not be as closed and secretive as Nasser's.

Style

In the beginning, Egyptians seemed to admire their leader. They praised his televised speeches, in which Sadat appeared "friendly and informal, even chatty."[48] He visited officers in the armed services and impressed them with his sincerity and concern for their welfare. They, in turn, vowed to back him should there be any danger to his rule.

His peasant upbringing pleased many Egyptians, too. While Nasser had also been born and raised in a small Egyptian village, he made little attempt during his rule to associate himself with the peasantry. But Sadat did. He made it a point to establish a base, as well as a vacation home, in his old village, Mit Abul-Kum. During speeches—especially during his frequent "fireside chats" on television—he would always refer humbly to his peasant upbringing.

Sadat proved an unassuming leader. This style was effective in disarming his critics in the civilian population. Many admired his respectful, even-tempered manner as a source of strength. His style kept the potential for political conflict to a minimum: it was hard to argue with a man who sought not to argue!

Sadat also came across as a good decision maker. Nasser had demanded detailed daily reports on messages from Egyptian ambassadors abroad, state security, financial matters, and food supply. Sadat, however, left details to subordinates to fret over. His concern was reserved for the major decisions that would affect the lives of all Egyptians.

Still, some criticized Sadat's focus on larger issues. They felt Sadat neglected the fine points of governing. Journalist Mohamed Heikal insists that Sadat was "by nature lazy . . . as far as paperwork was concerned." He also claims it was "significant that after he became President no official photographs were ever released showing him sitting at his desk."[49]

Jehan Sadat became an enormous asset to her husband in regard to such de-

Sadat visits Egyptian troops in November 1971.

tails. While Anwar spurned the tiresome reports that accumulated on his desk every day, Jehan, as journalist Mohamed Heikal claims, "did her best to make up for his omissions. She became an omnivorous reader of reports, showing a special predilection for transcripts of tapped telephone conversations and intelligence reports and for any matters which concerned the state of public opinion . . . though less interested in foreign affairs and economics."[50]

In time, though, some Egyptians found reasons to resent Anwar Sadat. They would accuse him of making promises he could not keep. For instance, for nearly three

A Helpful Spouse

In his book, Autumn of Fury: The Assassination of Sadat, *journalist and former minister of information in the Nasser regime, Mohamed Heikal recalls Jehan Sadat's efforts to help her husband in his new job:*

"She became an omnivorous reader of reports, showing special predilection for transcripts of tapped telephone conversations and intelligence reports and for any matters which concerned the state of public opinion, though less interested in foreign affairs and economics. . . . Jehan became Sadat's eyes and ears, and quickly gathered round her an entourage of her own—wives of businessmen, politicians, service officers, as well as ladies from the old aristocracy who had been leaders of society before the revolution. She paid particular attention to the officers of the Presidential Guard and their wives, and at one time arranged a marriage between one of the officers and her eldest daughter, though in the end it never came off."

According to journalist Mohamed Heikal, "Jehan became Sadat's eyes and ears."

During Sadat's rule, Jehan became an enormous asset by helping out with paperwork and other details of government.

years, he vowed to resolve the matter of the Sinai but did not. There was suspicion that other promises remained unkept as well. Sadat's government seemed to continue taping telephone conversations, even after Sadat declared, at least twice, that such tapes would be banned and burned. Finally, Egyptians grew weary of his attempts to identify with the peasantry. Sadat, after all, favored sophisticated pleasures such as pipes, expensive clothing, and American movies, especially westerns.

Soviets Out

Sadat himself had grown weary of the Soviet presence in Egypt. During Nasser's reign, Sadat had watched as capitalism was virtually swept out of the economy in the quest to become a model Communist state. Nasser appeared to have been interested in creating an ideal Communist state, in which all citizens would be provided for. But this had not quite worked out.

As the new president, Sadat's top priority was the general well-being of Egypt—by any means necessary. Early in his rule, Sadat decided he wanted the Soviets out of Egypt.

Sadat also had been unhappy with the way the Soviets had treated Nasser over the years—especially in regard to the constant delays in arms shipments. Consequently, Sadat was not shy in letting the world know of his dissatisfaction.

In addition, he had his own criticisms of Moscow. In 1971 he was angered over the attempted Soviet-backed Communist takeover of Sudan. Sadat did not want a Communist state on his border. The coup failed, and bitter feelings ran high between Sadat and Moscow.

One interested observer of all the growing tension between Moscow and Egypt was the United States. If the United States could woo Egypt away from the Soviet Union, the United States could achieve a better balance of power in the Middle East. Sadat knew very well that the United States wanted Egypt's alliance. He also knew that Egypt sorely needed the economic promise of an alliance with the United States.

To the bewilderment of the United States, however, Sadat signed a Treaty of Friendship and Co-operation with Moscow in late May 1971. It seemed hypocritical that Sadat would first discharge pro-Soviet ministers from his own government, then sign this agreement with their masters in Moscow. And if Sadat was so upset with the Soviet's shabby treatment of Egypt, why would he sign this type of accord with them? Not even Nasser had done such a thing.

But Sadat had good reasons for his surprising move. After signing the accord, Sadat let the word leak that if the United States forced Israel out of the Sinai, Egypt would immediately cut off relations with the Soviets. By signing the agreement Sadat was hoping to play one superpower against the other while driving a wedge between the Israeli-U.S. alliance.

Unfortunately for Sadat, the United States did not intend to sacrifice its relationship with Israel for a possible alliance with Egypt. While Sadat's plan did not work the way he had hoped, many critics deemed the move an example of masterful political thinking. And soon enough, the Egyptian leader would evict the Soviets from Egypt and create the opportunity for a relationship with the United States.

Before that day of eviction, however, more confrontations occurred between Sadat and the Soviets. Sadat, like Nasser, experienced the Soviets' faulty weapons and false promises. Throughout 1971 and into 1972, Sadat repeatedly requested

Sadat meets with Soviet leader Leonid Brezhnev and other officials in October 1971. To the surprise of the United States, Sadat had signed a Treaty of Friendship and Co-operation with Moscow the previous May.

weapons from the Soviets to use against Israel in the Sinai. Each time, the Soviets promised weapons but delivered nothing. They urged Sadat to be patient.

Finally, Sadat ran out of patience. In May 1972 newly elected U.S. president Richard Nixon and Soviet secretary general Leonid Brezhnev met in Moscow. Sadat vowed that if the two superpower leaders could not come up with a workable peace plan that would get Israel out of the Sinai, then Egypt would go to war to get the peninsula back.

Sadat sat back and waited. During their meeting, Nixon and Brezhnev generally agreed to cut tensions in the Middle East. In July 1972, Sadat still waited for his promised planes. Then he received the Soviet message asking him personally to "ease the tensions" between Egypt and Israel. There was no mention of getting the Sinai back and no mention of the long-awaited arms shipment.

Sadat was infuriated. He immediately summoned the Soviet ambassador and demanded that the Soviet presence in Egypt, numbering about fifteen thousand, be out of the country within a week. The Soviets thought Sadat was bluffing. The next day, Sadat ordered his war minister to implement the decision. By July 16, the Soviets were gone.

Ironically, once the Soviets were officially ousted from Egypt, they stepped up their arms deliveries. The Soviets finally realized they could lose all their influence in the Middle East to the United States. Between December 1972 and June 1973, weapons shipments poured into Egypt. As a result, Sadat exclaimed, "They are drowning me in new arms."[51] Sadat's bold move had proved to be a triumphant and fruitful one.

Getting the Sinai Back

From the very beginning of his rule, Sadat had promised that one way or another—whether by negotiation or by war—Egypt would get the Sinai Peninsula back from Israel. But getting back the Sinai was easier said than done. While 1971 had been deemed by Sadat to be "The Year of Decision," it passed without decisive action. But by 1973, Egyptians had become increasingly impatient. Despite Sadat's public assurances that he was serious about fighting Israel, he was not moving fast enough for some Egyptians. Students were especially upset with his lack of action. They protested and rioted, demanding the return of the Sinai. An Egyptian army captain led a convoy into a Cairo square, calling for immediate war. Journalist Mohamed Heikal remembers the mood of the country as being "one of frustration and anger."[52]

Outside of Egypt, however, Egypt was perceived as having lessened tensions between itself and Israel. The Israelis, for one, were impressed with Sadat's dismissal of Soviet personnel from Egypt. They seemed to believe that Egypt was saying it wanted no more war. This was not the case. As author George Sullivan wrote, "nothing could have been farther from the truth."[53] All the while, Egypt was on a countdown to war.

Chapter

5 The October War of 1973

Sadat believed that fighting for possession of the Sinai Peninsula was his duty. He knew that all Egyptians felt pride and prosperity would result from regaining the land that had been theirs. He also believed that with the Sinai back in Egyptian hands, Egypt would regain its sense of in-

In October 1972, Sadat declared that war with Israel was near. This photo shows U.N. forces stationed in Israeli-occupied Sinai to help prevent incidents between the feuding nations.

dependence and become an equal partner with Israel at any future peace talks.

Sadat claimed he attempted to think of peaceful means to get the Sinai back, but finally accepted war as his only option. Early in his rule, Sadat did in fact prolong a cease-fire agreement that Nasser had established with Israel. He also told a special U.N. envoy that he was willing to recognize Israel as a nation with its own political identity. He made appeal after appeal to the United Nations for the Sinai's return.

But Israel was not about to give back the Sinai for any Egyptian document that promised peace. Having been attacked verbally and militarily throughout their short existence, Israel did not trust Egypt or their other Arab neighbors to abide by any written agreement.

While Sadat talked about peace with Israel, he kept pushing for weapons from the Soviets. Sadat knew he really needed more than just a written agreement for the Egyptian people, even if it would get back the Sinai. He knew Egyptians wanted revenge for their losses in the wars of 1956 and 1967. He knew he needed to restore Egyptian pride, and this could be accomplished best on the battlefield. In his autobiography he wrote, "to cross into Sinai and hold on to any territory recaptured would restore our self-confidence."[54]

Confrontation

In preparation, the Egyptian armed forces tooled up for war. In late October 1972, General Ismail Ali had become commander in chief of the armed forces. His priority was to establish a plan of war against Israel. Soldiers in all branches of service were requested to offer their own ideas for a war with Israel. Author Fernandez-Armesto called this task "brilliantly calculated to maximize morale."[55] On December 28 of that year, Sadat went on Egyptian television to declare that war with Israel was near.

Author Fernandez-Armesto called the first eight months of 1973 "a countdown to war."[56] Early in the year, Sadat went on an all-out war of words against the Jewish state. He went on Egyptian television and announced "a state of total confrontation" with Israel.[57] A flood of anti-Semitic articles appeared in Egypt's popular magazines.

The Soviets offered their assistance to Egypt. In March 1973, Sadat sent General Ali to Moscow to renew ties and set up an arms deal. In the past the Soviet arms shipments would arrive months late, or not at all. But this time, the Soviets, eager to keep their influence in the region, carried on prompt and helpful negotiations. Almost overnight, Egypt received massive arms shipments.

Arab Unity

Sadat then turned to Israel's enemy in the north, Syria, for support. Syria's president, Hafez al-Assad, agreed to attack Israel si-

Syrian president Hafez al-Assad agreed to attack Israel simultaneously with Egypt.

multaneously with Egypt. Together, the two leaders set the day of attack: It was to be on the Jewish state's holiest day, Yom Kippur. Yom Kippur is the Jewish Day of Atonement, a day when all public services are suspended and most Israelis spend the day in fervent prayer. Sadat and Assad could not have picked a more advantageous day for an attack on the Jewish state.

Other Arab nations were especially eager to assist in the war effort against Israel. Lebanon, Tunisia, Algeria, and Morocco all agreed to provide troops and supplies. Sadat also kept in close and constant contact with representatives of King Faisal of Saudi Arabia. The Saudi king assured Sadat that Saudi Arabia's oil deliveries to Israel's allies in the West—especially the United States—would be cut back, as pun-

To assist in the war effort against Israel, King Faisal of Saudi Arabia threatened to cut back oil supplies to the West if they came to Israel's defense.

ishment, if they came to Israel's defense. At a conference of nonaligned nations in Algiers, Sadat also pressed other heads of state for Arab unity.

Sadat reestablished diplomatic relations with Jordan, another Arab state sharing a border with Israel. Sadat later wrote, "My clear and declared policy was that Egypt could not distinguish one Arab country from another on the basis of so-called progressive and reactionary or republican and monarchical systems. We should be committed to one thing only—our Arab character, pure and simple."[58]

Countdown

In May and August, Sadat used two tactics again and again. He threatened war against the Israelis, and he conducted civil defense drills in the cities and towns. These maneuvers alarmed Israel and

A Strategic Deception

In his autobiography, In Search of Identity, *Sadat recalls the ploy he used one month before his October 1973 surprise attack on Israeli forces in the Sinai:*

"In September the foreign minister of a certain European country called to see me. As part of my strategic deception I told him: 'Please convey this message to your President and ask him to keep it a secret, which should not be divulged. I am going to be at the UN headquarters in October 1973, but I don't want to announce this at the moment.' I knew that that report would be transmitted in a matter of minutes to Israel—and Israel came to believe, accordingly, that I wasn't planning to go to war."

caused them to rush troops and supplies to the border on a number of occasions. But the Israelis found no one there to fight. Sadat's bluffs became both costly and dispiriting for the Israelis. As Israel and the rest of the world pondered Egypt's action, Sadat did not show his hand.

As the days wound down, Sadat made final preparations to restore Egyptian pride and honor. A hint of how the war might progress, though, occurred on October 3—just three days before the scheduled attack on Israel. Sadat had summoned the Soviet ambassador and explained to him the plans for war. The ambassador consulted Moscow and then returned with a request. Would Sadat give his permission for four large transport planes to arrive from the Soviet Union and take their staff and civilians back to Russia? Author Sullivan wrote, "Sadat was dumbfounded. With war about to break out, the Soviets were fleeing the country. It was not a vote of confidence."[59] Sadat, though, was reportedly relaxed and confident.

General Hosni Mubarak commanded the Egyptian air force, which launched a surprise attack against Israeli positions on October 6, 1973.

War

According to plan, at precisely 2:00 P.M. on October 6, 1973, two hundred supersonic Egyptian jets darted across the Suez and struck at Israeli positions. Israeli forces were completely taken by surprise. An estimated 90 percent of all targets were hit in the first half-hour of attack, including aircraft and communications targets.

Sadat considered this initial attack a tremendous success. Egypt had lost only a few aircraft and had let loose a tremendous artillery barrage on their opponents. Sadat congratulated the air force commander, General Hosni Mubarak, for the success.

Then came a more dangerous undertaking: crossing the canal. Even in the very first hours of the war, Sadat felt he had accomplished much by letting his forces go to war. In fact, he was already philosophical about what might lay ahead. Mohamed Heikal remembers Sadat saying to him: "Whatever happens now, I have done my duty. If we are defeated in the Canal crossing, well, that's our fate. But the nation won't be able to blame me. We have to defend the honour of Egypt, whatever the cost, even if crossing the Suez Canal costs us twenty thousand casualties."[60]

The first Egyptians across the canal were swimmers. They had posed as

Israeli defense minister Moshe Dayan (center) and General Ariel Sharon (left) survey military operations at the Suez Canal during Sadat's campaign against Israel.

bathers but then suddenly swam together to the other side. Over a thousand commandeered rubber boats, armed with bazookas and portable missile launchers, backed them up. Using hastily constructed bridges held into place atop pontoon boats, the Egyptians filed over the canal north and south for over one hundred miles. They quickly stormed the massive Bar-Lev line, overwhelming Israeli forces and causing them to retreat. By nightfall, five divisions of Egyptian soldiers had crossed over into the Israeli-controlled Sinai Peninsula. The crossing of the Suez would later be referred to by Sadat as "a magnificent symphony played by tens of thousands of men."[61]

At the end of the first day of battle, Sadat received word from Moscow: the Soviets wanted him to agree to a cease-fire within 48 hours. Apparently, the Soviets were convinced that Egypt would eventually be the loser in the conflict, and they wanted to end the conflict before the tide

turned and damage was done to Egypt.

Sadat refused their request. Until he took all Egyptian land back, he told Moscow, he would not quit the battle. Moreover, he asked for new tanks from the Soviets. He wanted to use these in his campaign against the Israelis in the Sinai. There Israel was already suffering losses among its prized tank units. Sadat's stern stance towards Moscow now worked. The new tanks arrived in record speed, and Sadat quickly dispatched them to the Sinai to bolster his forces.

Success

The first days of the battle belonged to Egypt. While Syrian forces occupied Israeli forces at Israel's northern border—the Golan Heights—Egyptian forces marched east, across the Sinai. Israel suffered the loss of one-third of its air force on these two fighting fronts. By the end of the first week, Egyptian forces in the Sinai numbered over 1,000 tanks and 100,000 men. The Egyptian flag once again flew over the Sinai.

Other Arab nations offered their support. Kuwait, Saudi Arabia, and Tunisia all sent troops to help Egypt and Syria defeat Israel. Iraq moved tanks and more than 18,000 men to the Syrian front. King Hussein of Jordan ordered members of the Jordanian army to assist the Syrians.

In Israel, morale was at a low ebb. Israeli defense minister Moshe Dayan was dismayed by his own lack of preparedness for the war. He offered his resignation to Prime Minister Golda Meir, but she refused it. Meir herself, stunned by the rush of events, later recalled the early days of the October War as "a near disaster, a nightmare that I experienced and which will always be with me."[62]

At this point, Sadat was offered several cease-fire arrangements by the United States. President Nixon's secretary of state, Henry Kissinger, proposed that Sadat halt his attack and keep his troops behind the pre-October 6 boundary lines. Sadat refused. Then Kissinger suggested the lines be drawn to reflect Egypt's gains in the Sinai, past the Bar-Lev line. Again Sadat refused. He insisted that he would not stop his attack until Israel agreed to return all the territory it had won in the 1967 war.

Acclaim

The result of the first weeks' offensive restored pride to the Arab world. Never again would the world look on and laugh when Arab forces went to war.

Sadat's acclaim was tremendous. Egyptians now took great pride in their leader. Posters of Sadat lined the walls on buildings throughout Cairo. When foreign journalists rode through the streets, looking for public reaction to the war, they found Egyptians everywhere grinning and waving and yelling, "Victory for Sadat!"

Sadat himself was pleased with his accomplishment. In a speech to the Egyptian People's Assembly, he talked of a new day in Arab affairs, a new era of Arab strength and prominence in the world.

Admittedly unprepared for Egypt's surprise attack, Dayan—seen here with Israeli troops—attempted to resign from his post as defense minister.

Israeli armor crosses to the western bank of the Suez Canal as Israel spearheads into Egypt.

Arab forces, he said, had performed miracles at great risk and sacrifice. But the result was that "Our wounded nation has restored its honor, and the political map of the Middle East has been changed."[63]

The Tide Turns

Even as Sadat was delivering his address, Israel was making bold counterattacks. Four days after the beginning of the war, Israeli forces drove Syrian forces from the Golan Heights. The Israelis then proceeded to push well into Syria, stopping only twenty miles from the capital city, Damascus.

Israel displayed similar skill at counterattacking Egypt. Though a line of Egyptian men and tanks stretching north and south pushed Israeli forces east, there was

a hole in the line. A small force of Israelis rushed through that hole and hurried west, back toward the Suez Canal. On October 16, two hundred Israeli soldiers, led by General Ariel Sharon, crossed the Suez and landed on the Egyptian mainland. There they battled back a surprised Egyptian force. Then the bold Israelis fanned out north and south and interfered with supply and communication lines. They also attacked Egyptian missile installations.

Because the Israeli army only numbered about five hundred soldiers and the Egyptian army was much larger, the Egyptians were soon able to surround and contain them. The Egyptians did not massacre the Israelis because of the United States' firm commitment to Israel. The United States began supplying the Israelis with hourly satellite information on the location and movement of Egyptian troops. The United States also supplied them with an experimental TV-camera bomb. The bomb fixed on targets and destroyed them with deadly accuracy. Sadat feared he would lose his entire defense system and Israel would control the skies over Cairo and the rest of Egypt.

Embargo

Sadat then made his move. Upon Sadat's communication with Arab states in the oil-rich Persian Gulf, the Arab oil suppliers announced an immediate 5 percent cutback of their supplies to the Western backers of Israel, including the United States. King Faisal of Saudi Arabia also warned the Nixon administration that the embargo would last as long as it took Israel to give back the lands it occupied since the 1967 war and to acknowledge Palestinian Arab rights.

The oil embargo left millions of Americans suddenly panicked and inconvenienced—but also educated. Americans came to realize how their political support of Israel could cost them dearly at the gas station. While many Americans thought of the embargo as a kind of blackmail, public

Israeli soldiers in a military truck survey the body of a fallen Syrian soldier.

opinion swerved in favor of improving relations with the Arab states. Of course, this outcome was welcomed by the oil-producing nations.

Besides its effect on world oil supplies, the war had another effect on the international stage. The Soviet Union and the United States feared the conflict might eventually draw in each of them. With the United States backing Israel and the Soviets backing the Arab states, the two superpowers would be fighting against one another. With this concern in mind, a cease-fire was proposed by the Soviets and the Americans, and Egypt and Israel accepted it.

Settlement

Realizing it was useless to continue the conflict, Sadat agreed to allow Soviet and American officials to come to Cairo to help negotiate a firm settlement. Secretary of State Henry Kissinger was sent. Since the beginning of their acquaintance earlier, Kissinger and the Egyptian president had always been on friendly terms. Later, Sadat always referred to Kissinger as "my friend Henry." At that time, though, the two worked at finding a way to disengage the warring forces, and shortly thereafter a ceasefire arrangement was worked out. Fighting continued up until the date of the agreement, October 22. Then the war was over.

The October 22 cease-fire was short-lived, however. Two hours after it was issued, Israel advanced north and south farther into Egyptian territory. Sadat, outraged, saw this violation as a way to capture more land in order to have more strength in the peace talks to come.

Sadat had a message for Kissinger. If the Israelis did not move back to the lines of October 22, Egyptian forces would sur-

On November 7, 1973, U.S. secretary of state Henry Kissinger and Sadat meet for talks on the Middle East cease-fire.

Subtlety Eluded Him

Not everyone close to Sadat voiced acclaim for his ability as a leader. In a revealing passage from his book, Autumn of Fury: The Assassination of Sadat, *Mohamed Heikal referred to the surprise crossing of the Suez Canal by Israeli forces in 1973:*

"Part of the trouble was Sadat's own character. He had never had the education—or, indeed, the time—to give serious consideration to the problems which were going to confront him. He had no real understanding of Egyptian history. After a miserable childhood he had spent his adolescence and early manhood in underground adventures, and, once learned, conspiratorial habits are hard to shake off. He enjoyed the trappings of supreme power without appreciating the responsibilities which go with it. Nor did he understand the true nature of Egypt's relations with the rest of the Arab world. He saw that Egypt was a natural leader among the Arabs, but assumed that wherever she led the others would follow. The subtleties of leadership, the inevitable give-and-take demanded of it, completely eluded him."

round and annihilate the soldiers. Kissinger's response was simple: If Egypt moved in on the Israelis, America would fight on the Israeli side.

Before either side could make any further moves, the United Nations got involved. The organization sponsored talks to end the conflict that lasted on through November. In late December, a frustrated Sadat made secret plans to destroy the Israeli forces within their grasp. But Kissinger found out about the plan and urged Sadat to wait. Kissinger had had some success with speaking to the Israelis. He knew they might agree to a withdrawal on terms more favorable than Sadat would otherwise suspect.

Based on his conversation with Kissinger, Sadat agreed to wait for further developments. With this decision, Sadat acknowledged the role of the Americans in negotiating an Arab-Israeli peace. And this decision paid off. On January 18, 1974, Egypt and Israel signed a U.S.-sponsored agreement. The agreement stated that Israeli forces would move off the east bank of the Suez Canal; Egyptian troops would occupy a strip of land 5 to 7 ½ miles east of the canal; and U.N. forces would occupy a buffer zone separating Egyptian from Israeli forces, which retained control of the rest of the Sinai.

Analysis

With the October War officially ended, Egypt paused to consider its dead. Sadat never gave an official number of Egyptian casualties, but some experts estimate about six thousand lost their lives during the war.

Despite the high death toll, Egyptians believed they were victorious. They had gained back territory in the Sinai from Israel. Indeed, the crossing of the Suez alone was a display of Arab will and strength.

Egypt had also shown the rest of the world that Israel was not invincible. In Israel, the October War was known as the Yom Kippur War because it had begun on the Yom Kippur holiday. Approximately 2,500 Israeli soldiers were killed. In terms of their entire population, this was a huge loss. It would be like the United States losing over 150,000 soldiers in a war. The cost of destroyed Israeli equipment amounted to $2 billion.

By accepting Kissinger as the negotiator of the cease-fire, Sadat had also drawn the Americans into the conflict. This act established a precedent for American involvement in the Middle East peace process. At the same time, Sadat also made it clear to the United States what he wanted out of such negotiations. First among his demands was the return of the Sinai Peninsula and also the Gaza Strip, a small strip of land on the Mediterranean Sea northeast of the Sinai.

Finally, the 1973 war was necessary to Egypt if peace was to be obtained with honor. Before 1973, with only the history of the 1956 and 1967 shattering defeats, Egypt's peace would have been gained only by their submitting to Israel. Sadat

U.N. forces in Egypt. As part of the 1974 Arab-Israeli peace agreement, U.N. forces occupied a buffer zone separating Egyptian and Israeli forces.

felt that after 1973 Egyptians might get what they hoped for: political freedom and economic opportunities.

While it may seem suspicious to use war to achieve peace, Sadat was true to his word. Within a few days of the war's end, Sadat sent a representative to Washington, D.C., to work on a joint Egyptian-American initiative for peace.

6 Peace with Israel

In the wake of the war, the Arab world sang Sadat's praises. Many saw Anwar Sadat as a great Arab soldier, to be revered for Egypt's success against Israel. Many saw him as more than a victorious leader: One journalist said, "I never before believed in the role of the individual in history, but the hero, Anwar el-Sadat, is beyond my comprehension."[64]

Sadat holds the hand of King Faisal during a visit to Saudi Arabia in November 1973. After the war, Sadat's popularity swelled and he became a leader of the Arab world.

Anwar Sadat found himself a leader of the Arab world. At the Arab Summit held in November 1974, other Arab leaders listened attentively to Sadat when he told them that to go to war again with Israel would be a serious blunder. This was mainly due to America's commitment to the Jewish state. And peace with Israel would give Egypt and the other Arab nations the chance to direct their funds and various energies toward strengthening their economies.

But Sadat did not receive a positive response when he pressed for the United States to play a large role in the peace process. Sadat argued that only the United States had enough power to reason with Israel. Radical Arab leaders were displeased with this statement. Leaders like Qaddafi of Libya did not want to admit the United States had such power. Others, like Assad of Syria, were totally dependent on the Soviets for arms and aid. For them, dealing closely with the United States would only create friction with the Soviets.

Despite the protests of a few member nations, the summit resulted in a show of Arab unity. The Arab nations approved a continuation of the 1973 oil embargo against nations supporting Israel. They

When Anwar Sadat returned to Egypt after meeting with the Israelis, Egyptians in Cairo greeted him enthusiastically. As author Thomas Lippman reports, Egyptians were focused on one thing—peace:

"Egypt could no longer afford war. The Egyptians had nothing to look forward to if the struggle continued except more privation and suffering, and to what end? To please the Saudis and Kuwaitis, who were awash in wealth they were not sharing with Egypt? To support the Palestinians, who were killing other Arabs in Lebanon? To curry favor with the lunatic Qaddafi in Libya? No, it was the Egyptians who had done the fighting, who had driven the Israelis back from the Suez Canal, whole cities were in ruins, and they had had enough."

also voted to designate the Palestine Liberation Organization (PLO) as the sole representative of Palestinian Arabs. Sadat had much to do with the generally cooperative atmosphere at the summit.

Shortly after the summit, though, Sadat's leadership among the Arab nations fell almost as rapidly as it had earlier risen. Most of the fallout came from radical Arab leaders who blamed Sadat for accepting peace with Israel so quickly. They insisted that Sadat was in an extreme position of strength right after the war and could have made strong demands on Israel to hand over territory. Journalist Heikal wrote that Sadat had the oil embargo to use as leverage against the West, as well as the complete support of the Arab world and the Soviet Union. Despite these advantages, Heikal claims, Sadat

> turned his back on all this. Instead, he opted for the victory parades and the camera, and ignoring his Arab allies and friends, resolved that he would re-

build the area alone with his new friend, Henry Kissinger.[65]

Sadat was not terribly surprised at the criticisms from the Arab world and his fall from grace. He was quite satisfied with his victory. He clearly saw that peace with Israel could be in Egypt's future. With his pride nourished by the 1973 war, he set to work attending to Egypt's domestic ills. He was determined now to become a great leader for his people.

Visions of Greatness Sustain Him

Even as a youth, Anwar Sadat had seen himself as a man destined to do great things. At age fourteen, he fell into an irrigation ditch near his home in Mit Abul-Kum and nearly drowned. When later asked what his last thought was before he went under the water, he said: "If I drown,

Egypt will have lost Anwar Sadat."[66]

In 1975, to bolster his image as a great leader, he assigned Vice President Mubarak to write a new official history of the 1952 revolution. In the new version, Mubarak was to de-emphasize Nasser's role and highlight Sadat's.

Perhaps, though, it was a little too early to make claims of greatness. While the October War was a terrific success, desperate social and economic conditions persisted in Egypt. As time passed, other Arab leaders did not offer much help in the way of trade to Egypt. And Sadat's only reliable trading partner remained the Soviet Union—if that country could ever be called reliable.

The Opening

Eager to set Egypt's economy on the right track, Sadat began a program of economic development. Begun in 1974, he called

Sadat's vice president Hosni Mubarak set out to bolster Sadat's political image by writing a new history of the 1952 revolution.

this program *al-Infitah*, or "the Opening." The program was to be the economic equivalent of the military event of the 1973 war known as "the Crossing." The Opening would provide Egyptians with pride in their country and encourage them to work for a more prosperous Egypt.

The Opening would open up Egypt to Western and Arab investment. To bring in money from other countries, Sadat provided several enticements. First, Egyptian cities would offer free trade zones, or areas where goods could be imported and exported without being taxed. Second, cheap Egyptian labor would be available. Third, Egypt would repair and reconstruct its highways, bridges, and city streets for better transportation of goods.

Other aspects of the plan were geared toward aiding the battered economy. Tourism would be expanded, and the Sinai would be developed. (The western Sinai oil fields were returned to Egypt by Israel in an agreement signed October 10, 1975 and Egypt planned to put them to use.) Egypt would also work to improve relations with Arab countries. This would ensure that Egyptian workers already employed in Arab countries would be allowed to keep their jobs. These workers sent their salaries back to their families in Egypt, and this money was spent in the Egyptian economy.

The Failure of the Opening

In theory, the Opening was a noble undertaking. In practice, though, it was a failure. One problem was that the program was, in effect, the "Closing" for many corrupt members of Sadat's government. Officials from Nasser's day had benefited from business ventures controlled entirely by the government. With the new program, those officials would have to step aside, while private businesses were encouraged to fuel the Egyptian economy. Officials were reluctant to give up their control over their money-making interests. Though the officials stubbornly agreed to the Opening, they seemed to cause as much confusion and delay as possible. It seemed as if they wanted to retaliate against Sadat's new plan.

Another problem was that money from foreign investors was not wisely spent. Though efforts were made to shape up Egypt's facilities, these were too far gone to handle the upsurge in economic activity. Egypt's ports were too old-fashioned, its sewage systems overflowing, its streets pocked with potholes, and its pollution heavy. Businesspeople from wealthier countries found Egypt's cities to be intolerable places to conduct their affairs.

Egypt's poor also suffered under this failed policy. In large cities such as Cairo, the poor lived in ghettos and hovels. These were constantly being torn down in order to build tall office and luxury apartment buildings. The new structures were built for the expected flood of foreign businesspeople and workers arriving in Egypt. Many of the poor people were farmers who had left their land for the city because the land could no longer support them. Now many returned to their farms because they were abandoned by the city. Others continued to live in filthy conditions in the cities. Though it was designed to aid all Egyptians, the Opening actually increased the excesses of the rich upper class, hurt the poor, and led to greater corruption.

Egyptian Dissatisfaction

In 1976, despite their battered economy, Egyptians voted for Sadat's presidency for another six-year term. He had done much to instill pride in them where other lead-

Sadat attempted to stimulate Egypt's troubled economy by expanding private business and foreign investment. Here, Sadat meets with Saudi Arabian businessman Adnan Khashoggi.

Many Egyptian poor lived in ghettos in large cities such as Cairo, pictured here. Under the Opening, many of these areas were torn down to accommodate the expected flood of foreign businesspeople.

ers had failed. Of course, pride could not put a loaf of bread on the table. Even as Egyptians voted for their leader, grumbling and open resentment among them was growing.

In January 1977, Egyptians began to act out their dissatisfaction with Sadat's leadership by rioting over subsidy cuts on bread and beans. These two foods were staples in the Egyptian diet. For years the government had helped to keep the cost of these items low for the public by paying for a portion of the cost. However, Sadat cut the subsidies and the people's rage exploded. For thirty-six hours, Egypt's major cities were in chaos. Stores were broken into and looted. Fires were set and rail systems shut down. The army had to be dispatched to stop the violence. When it was over, more than eighty Egyptians were killed and thousands more were arrested.

Egypt appeared to be on the brink of civil war when Sadat stepped in with harsh measures. He issued emergency decrees suspending civil rights. He ordered mass arrests and, blaming the riots on the Communists, accused his old nemesis, Ali Sabri, of acting in conspiracy. Meanwhile, in the press and on television, Sadat repeatedly insisted that he had 99 percent of all Egyptians behind him. But the very fact that he had to take harsh measures, according to journalist Mohamed Heikal, "belied the claim."[67]

Truly, by mid-1977, Sadat's rule was in jeopardy. At this time, Egypt had debts of about $13 billion and was dependent on subsidies amounting to around $5 billion from the United States, Saudi Arabia, and other Arab states. The fact that Sadat had nine official residences at this time of general hardship did not sit well with the people, either. As author Patricia Aufderheide wrote, "These were difficult and dangerous times for Anwar Sadat."[68]

Gestures Towards Peace

Because of the desperation of his people, Sadat knew he must act quickly, or risk loss of power. Besides trying to come to grips with Egypt's troubled economy, he had been thinking about the one thing

that would make Egypt great and ensure that his own name would live on forever: making peace with Israel.

He had already done a few things to help decrease tensions with Israel since the end of the October War. With the help of Kissinger, disengagement treaties had been signed in 1974 and 1975. The reopening of the Suez Canal in June 1975 had been especially uplifting to Egypt. Sadat's message to the rest of the world had been that Egypt would take risks for peace.

Despite the controversy and lack of support from the Arab world, Sadat continued to nurture his working relationship with Henry Kissinger, the U.S. secretary of state under President Richard Nixon. Sadat felt a closeness with Kissinger that had been missing from his relationship with Secretary of State William Rogers. Rogers had held that position between 1969 and 1973. In his memoirs Sadat

Sadat shares a laugh with Henry Kissinger, U.S. secretary of state under Nixon. Kissinger and Sadat enjoyed an especially close personal relationship.

The Urbane Arab Leader

As Camelia Sadat points out in her book, My Father and I, *while U.S. secretary of state Henry Kissinger helped build her father's image in the West in the mid-1970s, Sadat himself did not necessarily change:*

"During Father's emergence as a world figure in the mid-1970s, I think that Henry Kissinger became a catalyst, perhaps unintentionally. In matters of foreign policy and in the international media, Kissinger helped build the image of President Sadat as a stable and reasonable person. Unfortunately, even now the Western press tends to stereotype Arab leaders as fanatical visionaries who are often self-serving and potentially volatile, unreliable, and dangerous. But in the company of Kissinger the world saw an urban Sadat who was well dressed, articulate—even in English—and possessed a sense of humor and the ability to handle the media. At that time the world did not know Father as a studious man who had been a communications specialist for most of his adult life."

Sadat's daughter Camelia wrote that Kissinger helped strengthen the image of a stable, articulate Sadat.

wrote about Kissinger: "For the first time, I felt as if I was looking at the real face of the United States, the one I had always wanted to see."[69]

The Soviets immediately expressed their disappointment over Sadat ignoring them and talking to the Americans. They had been disappointed with Sadat before. Sadat had kicked out the pro-Soviet opposition in Egypt, as well as Soviet military and civilians. He had rejected Moscow's advice about going to war with Israel.

Sadat chats with U.S. president Jimmy Carter. Because they had much in common, the two leaders developed a special rapport.

Sadat, however, went his own way and continued strengthening his relationship with the United States through Kissinger. The Soviets, fed up and frustrated, halted arms shipments to Egypt and condemned its leader.

Changing His Thinking

When Nixon resigned the presidency and Vice President Gerald Ford took Nixon's place, communication between Sadat and Washington became a little bumpy. Ford was not viewed as a powerful world leader, for he had not been elected to the presidency. But the bumps were smoothed away when the Carter administration took over in 1976.

U.S. president Jimmy Carter and Anwar Sadat found that they had much in common with one another. Both men were deeply religious, and both men had a love of the earth, of working with their hands, of building and growing. They came to respect and trust one another.

When Carter sent Sadat a long, detailed letter putting forth his own views on the complicated world of the Middle East, Sadat studied the letter and withdrew. He took solitary walks by the Nile, thinking about the great barriers that stood between Arabs and Israelis.

At this time—October 1977—Sadat also paid a visit to Romania. Though under the influence of the Soviet Union, Romania had good relations with Israel. Romanian leader Nicolae Ceausescu told Sadat the Israelis wanted peace. Not only that, said Ceausescu, but the Israeli prime minister, Menachem Begin, was a leader who could deliver on a peace agreement. This surprised Sadat, who saw Begin as a hardline leader unwilling to compromise.

Sadat returned to Egypt. He remembered the important lesson he had learned back during his imprisonment in Cell 54: "He who cannot change the very fabric of his thought will never be able to change reality, and will never, therefore, make any progress."[70] He decided he had to rely on that lesson.

Then Sadat had a kind of vision. He could see himself praying at al-Aqsa Mosque in the old city of Jerusalem. Al-Aqsa Mosque is the third holiest site in the Arab world, behind Mecca and Medina, in Saudi Arabia. With this vision, it became clear to Sadat that he might achieve a breakthrough in the peace process if he went to Israel and spoke with the Israelis on their own soil.

It was a tremendous breakthrough in his own thinking—and a quick one, too. Just a few months before, in February, he had declared to the Egyptian press that as long as there was even one Israeli soldier on Egyptian land, "I am not ready to contact anyone in Israel at all."[71] Now, Anwar Sadat had different thoughts on the matter.

Responses

Sadat told the Egyptian people of his plans. But few believed Sadat's words when he announced, "I am willing to go to the ends of the earth if this will prevent one soldier, one officer, among my sons from being wounded, not being killed, just wounded."[72] They thought he was exaggerating—especially when he said that he would even visit Israel, Egypt's sworn enemy. But Sadat was serious. He assured skeptics that he meant what he said, and he began to plan for his trip.

Messages revealing Sadat's plans were sent to various governments, including Israel and the United States. Sadat told his own parliament: "Israel will be astonished when it hears me saying now before you that I am ready to go to their house, to the Knesset itself, and to talk to them."[73] (The Knesset was Israel's ruling government body.) Soon afterward he declared to skeptics, "I am going to Jerusalem, and the other [Arab leaders] will have to follow in line."[74]

While many in the Arab world wondered at Sadat's motives, many were displeased. In Cairo, posters of Sadat wearing stars and stripes and an eyepatch (as did Israeli defense minister Moshe Dayan) appeared throughout the city. In Syria, a day of mourning for Sadat's decision was declared.

The Israeli government was suspicious, too, at first. Prime Minister Menachem Begin, member of the conservative Likud party, at first expressed his doubts. Begin himself had been an underground revolutionary in the years leading up to Israel's rebirth after World War II. For years, Begin and Sadat had openly expressed their dislike for one another.

But soon Israel voiced its optimism. Its leaders did not want to miss the opportunity and quickly sent Sadat an invitation to come and speak before the Knesset. Sadat promptly accepted the invitation.

Events moved along quickly, and Egyptians were amazed. They found it hard to believe what was happening. Just before the fifty-eight-year-old Sadat climbed aboard his official government

(Left) In a bold move toward peace with Israel, Sadat meets with Israeli prime minister Menachem Begin. (Below) Upon his arrival in Israel, Sadat is greeted by an honor guard at Ben-Gurion International airport.

plane to depart for Jerusalem, one of his aides was heard to say, "Either this man is mad, or he is truly great."[75]

History Is Made

On November 19, 1977, at 8:03 P.M., Anwar Sadat arrived in an Egyptian Air Boeing 707 jet at Ben-Gurion International Airport. Yitzhak Rabin, in his book *The Rabin Memoirs*, remembers the moment Anwar Sadat appeared in the doorway of the plane. "Our emotion peaked in a way I had not thought possible. It was a uniquely electric moment for us all; one of those moments that remain etched in your memory forever; the kind that people call upon to date a generation."[76]

Sadat, wearing a gray-checked suit and silvery tie, stepped off the plane and onto Israeli territory. A military band played the Egyptian national anthem, followed by the Israeli anthem, *Hatikva*. In the back-

ground, gunners fired off a 21-gun salute. The sounds of cameras clicking and questions shouted issued from the over one thousand foreign reporters covering the event. Prime Minister Begin was the first to officially greet Sadat. "Thank you," said Sadat, shaking hands. Begin responded, "It's wonderful to have you. Thank you for coming."[77]

On his way to his limousine, Sadat shook hands with Israel's most powerful political leaders, gathered there to meet him. He was greeted by former prime minister Golda Meir, former prime minister Yitzhak Rabin, and General Ariel Sharon, who had led the daring raid west across the Suez Canal during the 1973 war.

Sadat arrived at Jerusalem's King David Hotel. In 1946 Menachem Begin, as leader of the underground Irgun organization, had bombed the hotel as part of a campaign to get the British presence out of Palestine. Soon after Sadat's arrival, Begin went to pay him a courtesy call. The visit was short—only about half an hour. But Begin emerged from the hotel, grinning and telling reporters, "I can say that we like each other."[78]

Israelis were in a state of shock over what was happening before their eyes. In Jerusalem, *Time* magazine bureau chief Don Neff observed that "people were stopping conversations in midsentence, nonplused. Husbands and wives stared at each other in disbelief. Knots of people gathered on the streets and in shocked tones tried to figure out what it all meant. The unbelievable was happening."[79]

In Israel, Sadat visits al-Aqsa, an important mosque in the old city of Jerusalem.

A Speech for Peace

Early the next day, Sadat first went to al-Aqsa, the mosque in the old city of Jerusalem. There he fulfilled the private vow he had recently made. The Egyptian leader prostrated himself in prayer at one of the most sacred places in Islam. In a show of respect for the Christian religion, he then visited the nearby Church of the Holy Sepulchre, where Jesus Christ is said to have risen from the dead. After that, he visited Yad Vashem, Israel's memorial to the six million Jews murdered in the Holocaust.

At four o'clock in the afternoon, Sadat stood before the Israeli Knesset. Government officials and reporters awaited his words with excitement and curiosity. He began his fifty-seven-minute speech (in Arabic) by cordially addressing the Israelis. He told them he welcomed the opportunity to live in peace with them.

He went on to say that certain demands had to be met, though, for Egyptians and Israelis to live in peace. First, all Arab territories controlled by Israel had to be given up. Second, the rights of Arabs who resided in Palestine had to be acknowledged by Israel. These Arabs, he declared, also deserved the right for a state of their own.

Finally, Sadat did what all Arab leaders before him had refused to do: he recognized the existence of the state of Israel. He also recognized a basic desire shared by all nations of the world: the desire for peace and security. "Today we agree to live with you in permanent peace and justice. Israel has become an accomplished fact recognized by the whole world and the superpowers. We welcome you to live among us in peace and security."[80]

While the speech was met with hearty applause, it did not indicate much of a change in Sadat's political stance toward the Jewish state. But the mere fact that an Arab enemy of the Jewish state had come to offer peace was enough of a reason to celebrate.

Abba Eban, former Israeli foreign

Sadat meets with Knesset members. Sadat's historic visit paved the way for diplomatic relations between Egypt and Israel.

Throngs of Egyptians greet their leader on his return from Israel. In the words of Thomas Lippman, Sadat brought with him "hope for peace and a better life."

minister and a speaker of Arabic, commented, "The speech itself was predictable. I could have written it myself. But the Middle East can never be the same again."[81] Further, Eban remarked that Israel "suddenly underwent a total transformation. At last the windows were opened and the air came rushing in."[82]

Response

Back in Egypt, Sadat met with resounding support. In Cairo, Egyptians who, often in awe and wonder, had watched their leader on television, now welcomed him home. Sadat told his people that the great barriers dividing his country and Israel had been shaken, and peace was in the future.

As Thomas Lippman recalled, "Now hope was restored—hope for peace and a better life. Sadat was bringing it with him from Jerusalem, and the people turned out to say yes: yes to peace with Israel, yes to ending the long fruitless struggle that had exhausted their country and killed their sons."[83]

The world responded in favorable terms as well. Most importantly, many nations—mainly from the West—viewed Anwar Sadat as a true world leader. They saw him as a man who could help replace the threat of war with the security of real, lasting peace. An Egyptian journalist wrote, "By making this journey Sadat crossed the sound barrier between the normal and the abnormal, between the thinkable and the unthinkable. Jerusalem made Sadat a superstar."[84]

7 Revolution of the Spirit

Not everyone was impressed by Sadat's trip to Jerusalem. Many in other Arab countries cried out, as if struck by a personal blow. Syria declared the day of Sadat's visit to Jerusalem a national day of mourning. In Palestinian refugee camps outside Damascus, Syria, photographs of Sadat were burned in bonfires. Demonstrations against Sadat's trip broke out in Beirut, Tripoli, and Baghdad. Saudi Arabia charged Sadat with breaking the unified Arab front against the Jewish state. Among the Arab states, only Oman, Morocco, Tunisia, and the Sudan voiced support for Sadat.

Momentum

The Israelis were pleased by Sadat's overture and intended to keep up the momentum for peace. However, they were not terribly pleased about Sadat's demands, especially his solution to the displacement of Palestinian Arabs. But soon after Sadat's trip to Israel, Prime Minister Begin of Israel went to Egypt.

The meeting, held in the Suez Canal city of Ismailia, was disappointing. To Sadat, Begin did not seem to want to really talk about the possibility of peace. In ne-

Sadat and Begin shake hands as they leave a press conference following their talks in Ismailia. Disappointed, Sadat later called Begin "an obstacle to peace."

With Jimmy Carter looking on, Sadat and Begin meet at the Camp David presidential retreat.

gotiations, he found the Israeli prime minister unwilling to compromise. Frustrated, Sadat told the world press that the Israeli leader was "an obstacle to peace."[85] Begin returned to Jerusalem a few days later, accompanied by a cloud of gloom that spread over the country.

One major stumbling block in Israel's talks with Egypt was a disagreement over the rights to the West Bank. The West Bank was a piece of land extending less than a hundred miles north and south from the city of Jerusalem. The Jordan River was its eastern border. Prior to the 1967 war, this chunk of land, including half of Jerusalem, belonged to Jordan. Israel had captured the West Bank in the war and still refused to give it up.

Camp David

To the surprise of many, President Carter asked Sadat and Begin to come to the United States to resume the quest for Middle East peace. The two leaders were invited to the presidential retreat at Camp David in the Catoctin Mountains of Maryland, about seventy miles from Washington, D.C. Sadat and Begin accepted the invitation, and in September 1978, they traveled to America to talk about their agreements and differences. In the mountains together for eleven days, the trio of world leaders—one a Jew, another a Christian, the third a Moslem—reasoned, argued, and prayed together.

At first, communication between Begin and Sadat at Camp David was frustrating. Sadat complained repeatedly that Begin was impossible to negotiate with. Jehan Sadat recalled a conversation she had with her husband several days after the meetings at Camp David had begun. "I am leaving Camp David. . . . Begin is being totally unreasonable. He refuses to return the West Bank to Arab rule. . . . There is no point in continuing. All that we have worked for is finished."[86] Jehan convinced her husband to give it one more try, though, and, with much assistance from President Carter, the meetings proceeded.

Finally, some points began to be negotiated. Israel conceded that the Sinai Peninsula belonged to Egypt, and that it could be given back. Israel also agreed to

After long and often frustrating negotiations, Carter announced the creation of the Camp David Accords. Below, the trio that had taken such momentous steps toward peace.

build a highway at its southernmost tip, in the port city of Eilat. The highway would allow vehicles to travel easily from the Sinai into Jordan. Thus a bridge between North Africa and Arabia would be established.

Agreement

Sadat also agreed to several points. First, once the Sinai was back in Egyptian hands, it would be demilitarized. Only one division of Egyptian troops and a U.N. peacekeeping force would be allowed on the mutual border between Egypt and Israel. This would allay Israeli fears of a surprise Egyptian attack. Second, Sadat agreed to full acceptance and recognition of the state of Israel. The economic boycott of Israel would end, and Israeli ships would be allowed to pass through the Suez Canal. Also, Israel would be permitted to buy oil from the Egyptians.

Finally, both sides agreed to work toward solving the question of Palestinian Arab independence. Though no timetable was set, this agreement was meant to satisfy not only the two countries but the rest of the Arab world as well as the Palestinian Arabs.

The United States proved to be a generous mediator. Israel had agreed to give back some of the oil fields it had developed in the Sinai, even though these wells gave Israel about 25 percent of its required oil supplies. To ease the potential shortage this might create, the United States promised to give Israel supplies of oil if the Jewish state ever needed them. Also, the United States promised to help finance the construction of two new air-

The Appeal of Peace

In his book, Sadat and His Statecraft, *author Felipe Fernandez-Armesto contends that the Egyptian leader was propelled toward making peace by his deep religious faith and "fine-tuned morality," which issued from Sadat's faith in Islam:*

"Islam is the religion of *jihad,* of the Holy War waged unremittingly for the sake of the faith, but it is no crude warrior-creed—as some westerners believe or purport to believe; Sadat's Mohammedanism [Islam] belonged to the mystical tradition, in which the *jihad* is internalized and transformed into an inward psychomachia, fought against doubt and lust and petulance and caprice and all the inner demons of one's own evil conscience. We have already seen how much of his language is suffused with the glow of faith; in no context was the rolling landscape of Sadat's speech more thickly wooded with religious images than when he was speaking of peace. He talked of the duty of sparing coming generations from suffering for which God will call warmongers of the present age to account."

ports in Israel's Negev Desert, south of Jerusalem. These would replace the three airports built in the Sinai. The United States would also provide both Egypt and Israel with billions of dollars in additional military and economic support.

The World Responds

At the end of the momentous eleven days, Jimmy Carter announced to the world the creation of the Camp David Accords. Leaders from around the world expressed acclaim for the three men. All over the world, photos of Carter, Begin, and Sadat and their wives smiling and joking with one another, even hugging one another, captivated the imagination. Sadat and Be-

gin were further acclaimed and rewarded when they were both awarded the Nobel Peace Prize on October 27, 1978. It had become apparent, then, that peace was possible after all—even between the bitterest of enemies.

But the work was not over yet. The next few months were spent ironing out the details of the formal treaty between the two countries. Finally, in March 1979, Carter flew to Jerusalem and Cairo with completed proposals. These were accepted by Begin and Sadat. Later that month, on March 26, a ceremony was held on the White House lawn in Washington, D.C. At the ceremony, Begin and Sadat signed the historic document, putting an end to the hostilities which had plagued the two countries since the birth of Israel thirty years before.

On March 26, 1979, Sadat, Carter, and Begin stand at attention during the peace treaty signing ceremony on the White House lawn.

Returning once more to Cairo after a controversial trip, Sadat received an enthusiastic Egyptian response. Five days after the signing of the historic peace treaty, thousands of Egyptians—clapping, singing, dancing, and shouting out his name—met Sadat at the airport. His motorcade to Cairo followed a route lined by an estimated two million people. Pictures of Sadat were everywhere. His image had even been woven into rugs for display and souvenirs. Author George Sullivan reported that Sadat was then considered the "architect of a new Mideast."[87]

Hostility

Despite the Egyptians' enthusiasm, Egypt still suffered from overpopulation, disease, unemployment, and illiteracy.

Moreover, several groups within Egypt expressed their displeasure with Sadat. A former member of the original Free Officer's Association worried that the accords would allow Israeli infiltration into aspects of Egyptian society. They were also concerned that the Sinai would ultimately belong to the Americans, not the Egyptians.

Some considered the signing of the accords a "surrender" to Israel and the West. Fundamentalist groups in Egypt considered the signing a treachery and betrayal.

Other Arab nations also predictably reacted with hostility. Libya and Syria refused to accept the accords. Saudi Arabia, fearing criticism by more radical nations, followed suit. In November 1978, several leaders of Arab nations meeting in Iraq decided to offer Sadat $5 billion per year for ten years if he did not sign the agreement with Israel. Sadat publicly refused the bribe.

Arab nations became hostile to Sadat and declared diplomatic boycotts of Egypt. Once the leading member of the influential Arab League, Egypt found itself outside the fold, banished from the organization. The Arab League headquarters moved from Cairo to Tunis, Tunisia. Arab nations declared economic boycotts of Egypt, too. Suddenly, Egypt found itself expelled from the powerful Organization of Petroleum Exporting Countries (OPEC).

Peace Process Stalls

The peace process between Egypt and Israel, begun with so much promise, was now stalled. The Israelis were willing to part with the Sinai Peninsula. This was not a problem. The Sinai was a tremendous expanse of land, far from Israel's large cities and, because of its size, difficult to defend.

On the other hand, Israel made it clear they were not about to give up the West Bank, captured from Jordan in the 1967 war, for the creation of a Palestinian Arab state. To give up the West Bank, they reasoned, would be to give up land—close to the center of Israel—to a people who were hostile to the Jewish state. Such a transfer would put Israel in mortal danger.

Sadat was outraged when Israel continued to build Israeli settlements on the West Bank. He believed the buildup defied the Camp David Accords, which called for future Palestinian Arab autonomy. One U.S. diplomat noted the difference between the two leaders' meaning of the word autonomy: "For Sadat, autonomy is a millimeter or so short of full sovereignty. For Begin, it is barely a millimeter beyond what exists now."[88]

Fundamentalism on the Rise

With the peace process bogged down, Sadat turned his complete attention toward Egypt's economy. Yet, in the years that followed, Egypt's economic situation did not improve. Inflation, as well as overpopulation, grew at numbing rates. When bread shortages occurred in 1980, Sadat desperately tried to solve the problem by raising salaries of government employees and cutting the prices of some foods.

Sadat began to grow concerned, too, about the rising tide of Islamic fundamentalism in his country. Islamic fundamentalists are violently opposed to the West. He knew Islamic fundamentalists throughout the Arab world felt betrayed that he had shown himself as an ally of the West—especially of the United States. "It was religious fanaticism, more than any other single factor, that stalled and thwarted Sadat's work, imperiled his regime and at last destroyed his life," wrote author Felipe Fernandez-Armesto.[89]

Religious fundamentalists had their

own reasons to be angry. They watched Sadat back U.S. efforts to either support or overthrow governments in various parts of the Middle East and Africa, including Chad, Somalia, and Morocco. They watched Sadat kiss Rosalynn Carter in public (displays of public affection between men and women are forbidden by Islamic law) and tolerate the sale and production of pork (also considered taboo by Islamic law). Added to that, according to author Thomas Lippman in his book, *Egypt After Nasser*, Sadat "made peace with the Zionist occupiers of Jerusalem, and prayed at al-Aqsa Mosque while it was under the control of infidels."[90]

The fundamentalists also watched as Sadat, in January 1979, took in the exiled and ailing shah of Iran, Mohammed Reza Pahlavi. The exiled shah, who had helped Sadat during the October War, had been recently overthrown by Islamic fundamentalists. Moreover, when the shah died, Sadat gave him a lavish funeral. For his allegiance to the West and its customs, Sadat received money and arms. From Arab fundamentalists throughout the Arab world and in his own country, he received nothing but anger and contempt.

In 1981, Sadat made moves to appease the small but growing and well-organized factions of Islamic fundamentalists in his country. He approved legislation that made it illegal to challenge popular religious and moral values in public. For example, women whose dresses did not reach their ankles were punished under this law, known as the "Law of Shame." He also increased censorship and made Islamic law, known as *Shari'a*, which is based on religious principles, the basis for all new legislation.

Sadat made other moves to try to preserve his presidency. He made himself president for life. In 1981, rioting broke out between fundamentalists and Christian Copts, and Sadat used the situation to arrest 1,500 of his opponents, including Muslim fundamentalists. He also declared himself his own prime minister. Finally, he became desperate enough about the turmoil arising out of the terrible economic mess in Egypt that, in a 1981 meeting with Western bankers, he signed an agreement pledging revenues from the Suez Canal and the Sinai oil fields in exchange for

Many Islamic fundamentalists felt betrayed by Sadat when he made peace with Israel. New tensions flared when, in January 1979, Sadat offered political asylum to the shah of Iran (left), who had been overthrown by fundamentalists.

Living His Faith

After offering political asylum to the ailing shah of Iran and incurring the wrath of Muslim fundamentalists opposed to the shah, Jehan Sadat, in her book, A Woman of Egypt, *notes with anger the fundamentalists' charge that her husband was a traitor:*

"Now the fanatics were calling my husband a kafir, an infidel, for continuing this tradition of hospitality and support. How wrong they were. No one had a deeper faith than Anwar. He knew the Holy Book by heart, and every Ramadan he read it again three times, recording it once for our children. He slept with a Quran under his pillow, kept another on his bedside table, and had a verse from the Quran inscribed on the back of his watch. He missed none of the day's five prayers, prostrating himself so often that he had the mark of the devout on his forehead, the small circular bruise Egyptians call el-zebida, 'the raisin.'. . . Most importantly, Anwar lived his faith, abiding always by the principles of Islam."

badly needed loans. Still, threats to his regime and to his life became more and more commonplace.

Years before, Egypt and the United States had established precautions to protect the Egyptian leader. The United States, for example, had spent an estimated $25 million on security training, communications, and weapons systems designed to guard Sadat's life. In 1974, President Nixon had personally given Sadat a $2 million armored helicopter as a gift. But all the precautions to protect Sadat's life would ultimately fail.

Assassination

The morning of October 6, 1981, Anwar Sadat was feeling a little nervous. He was scheduled to review a military parade on the outskirts of Cairo in a suburb called Victory City. This was an annual military parade celebrating the Egyptian effort in the 1973 October War.

At the parade, nothing seemed out of the ordinary. Sadat, dressed in his blue and white military uniform and his brown leather boots, was flanked by officials in his government, including Vice President Hosni Mubarak.

Two hours passed with the usual pageantry of the occasion, but as Sadat stood to address his men, something strange happened. One of the army trucks came to a short stop before the reviewing stand. A soldier in khakis and a blue beret ran up to the stand. Sadat at first smiled, perhaps thinking this was all part of the planned spectacle. Sensing something wrong, though, Sadat, despite the efforts of one of his bodyguards, moved in sight of the soldier, as if in defiance of his assas-

On October 6, 1981, Sadat was assassinated while reviewing a military parade in Cairo.

sins. It was his last act of defiance.

The soldier, later identified as Lieutenant Khaled al-Islamboulie, tossed a grenade into the stand. Other men, clutching submachine guns, leaped out of the truck and opened fire. Sadat was the target, and the bullets found their mark. Sadat fell in a group of overturned chairs, as others in the stand either ran or hid for cover. Sobhi Abdel Hakim, president of the council of elders, was in the reviewing stand and fell to the floor as the assassins fired. "I was amazed," he reported, "when I found myself face to face with the President on the floor, his whole face covered in blood."[91]

A helicopter rushed the blood-drenched body of Sadat to nearby Maadi Hospital. Vice President Hosni Mubarak, who had been seated beside Sadat, had escaped without injury. Mubarak waited for the official word from the surgeons laboring over the dying president. Late in the afternoon, the word came at last: The president of Egypt was dead.

A Man Ahead of His Time

In the wake of the assassination of Anwar Sadat came varied reactions. U.S. president Ronald Reagan called the murder "an act of infamy, cowardly infamy," which "fills us with horror."[92] Former president Jimmy Carter called Sadat the greatest leader he had ever met and praised him for doing more for peace in the world than anyone else in this century.

In the Arab world, Sadat's murder was cause for celebration. Libyan radio got hold of the story immediately and, in de-light, went over the details of the killing. Libyans even danced in the streets of their cities. In fact, there were a large number of car accidents, as drivers became reckless with delight. Syrian and leftist Lebanese voiced their pleasure at the news. The Palestine Liberation Organization was exuberant. This group had been created in the 1960s in order to establish a Palestinian Arab state in Palestine. They also had orchestrated many terrorist attacks against Israel and throughout the Middle East in

In the streets of Cairo, two Egyptian women mourn the death of their slain president.

Grief etches the face of Sadat's widow as she meets with former U.S. presidents Jimmy Carter (left) and Gerald Ford (right).

support of this goal. On the West Bank, happy shopkeepers passed out free candy.

The media in Iran and Libya cried out harshly for the Egyptian people to rise up against Sadat's successors and replace the government with an Islamic Fundamentalist regime. But Egyptians responded with perplexing quiet to the death of Sadat. There were no government or military protests. Throughout the country, the streets were deserted. This was a stark contrast to the response of Egyptians years before, upon the death of Nasser. Then crowds thronged the streets, pushing and shoving, calling out the dead leader's name.

Funeral

The funeral was held a few days later. Representatives from Great Britain, France, and Germany paid their respects, as did Israeli prime minister Menachem Begin. Prominent politicians from the United States also came to express their grief. While Ronald Reagan could not attend, due to security concerns, three former U.S. presidents arrived to express their grief: Jimmy Carter, Gerald Ford, and Richard Nixon. Secretary of State Alexander Haig and Secretary of Defense Caspar Weinberger represented the United States, too, as well as Henry Kissinger, the man whom Sadat had called "my good friend Henry." In all, representatives from over eighty countries arrived in Egypt to bid farewell to Anwar Sadat.

At the funeral, members of the Arab League were conspicuously absent. Only three countries—the Sudan, Oman, and Somalia—out of the twenty-four countries that made up the league sent representatives to the funeral.

On the day of the funeral, security precautions were in evidence. Police sharpshooters took up positions on rooftops. An extraordinary number of police and soldiers were assigned to protect the funeral procession. The government also anticipated crowds pouring into the streets to show their grief, and these crowds would have to be contained.

But on this day, crowd control would not be necessary. According to authors David Hirst and Irene Beeson, lines of policemen "stood with arms locked as if to hold back a crowd. But there was no crowd."[93]

One reason for the deserted streets is that after the assassination, a state of emergency had been announced. Taking precautions against the possibility of an uprising, Mubarak declared that any five people gathered on a street would be subject to arrest and questioning.

But it is also true that Egyptians were not terribly surprised or shocked by Sadat's assassination. Many thought he had gone too far by making peace with Israel. Retaliation had seeemed a certainty. Many Egyptians, upset with Sadat for various reasons, felt that Sadat had gotten what he deserved.

Amid tight security, a caisson drawn by six horses took the casket containing the remains of Anwar Sadat to a sarcophagus in Egypt's Tomb of the Unknown Soldier. There, he was laid to rest—right across from the reviewing stand where he had been gunned down. The funeral party left behind a black marble tombstone inscribed with an epitaph Sadat himself had suggested only a few years before: "President Mohammed Anwar Sadat, hero of war and peace. He lived for peace and he was martyred for his principles."[94]

A caisson bears the coffin of Sadat during his funeral on October 10, 1981. Heavy security kept crowds away from the processional route.

Honoring Sadat's Legacy

After the assassination, the Egyptian Parliament quickly nominated Vice President Hosni Mubarak to the presidency by a vote of 330-0. A public referendum then confirmed Mubarak's position as the new Egyptian president.

Would Mubarak keep Egypt on the path of peace, or would Egypt be led back toward an enemy stance against Israel? The world looked to Hosni Mubarak to continue the innovations of Anwar Sadat. And the world was quickly assured of Mubarak's intentions: "Camp David is Camp David," the new president told *Newsweek*. "We are going to respect our word, the peace treaty and normalization."[95]

The new president dealt quickly with Sadat's assassins. Lieutenant Islamboulie,

After Sadat's assassination, Vice President Hosni Mubarak became president by public referendum.

head of the murder squad, had been part of an underground religious extremist network operating in Egypt. Islamboulie, the three gunmen involved in the assassination, and twenty others charged as their accomplices were all tried by a military court in November 1981. All twenty-four were found guilty, and all were executed five months later in April 1982.

After Sadat

After Sadat's death, there were no other breakthroughs regarding the peace process in the Middle East. The peace with Israel remained—and remains up to this day. However, tensions occur now and then over various disputes and conflicts. Despite Sadat's prediction, no other Arab nations followed his lead and made peace with the Jewish state.

Also, the political freedoms Sadat established in Egypt have been restrained due to a rise in religious tensions. Hosni Mubarak still presides over Egypt, but his rule has been shaken by rising fundamentalism in Egyptian society. As author Thomas Lippman wrote in 1989, "Egypt seems to be waiting for something dramatic to happen."[96] As this book goes to press, religious tensions are high not only in Egypt but throughout the Middle East.

Yet there have been positive developments. After the Persian Gulf War of 1990, the victorious allied coalition of nations, which included Egypt and Syria, sat down with Israel for a fresh round of peace talks. This marked the first time Syria, Palestinian Arabs, and Israel ever agreed upon such an encounter. In mid-1993, the world watches and waits for serious developments to come out of the talks.

Sadat's Legacy

Sadat, for all the controversy he generated, remains known as a courageous figure for his attempts to make peace with Israel.

"Peace," wrote Fernandez-Armesto, "even when his popularity was waning, was the most popular of Sadat's policies in Egypt."[97]

His momentous efforts had a tremendous effect throughout the Arab world as well. Many were negative, of course. However, in the long run, Sadat will be remembered for his monumental visit to Israel, which shattered the myth that had kept the Middle East at war since the creation of the state of Israel: that Israelis and Arabs could never negotiate face to face.

With his trip to Jerusalem, Sadat had proven his reputation as a risk taker. Early in his career he had plotted against King Farouk and the British forces in Egypt. Later, as president, he infuriated the Soviets by expelling eighteen thousand of their advisors from Egypt. In 1973, he sent forty-five thousand Egyptian soldiers across the Suez Canal in a lightning attack on powerful Israel. Finally, in 1977, he himself went to Israel to try to make peace. Who knows what other risky moves he might have made, in the name of peace, had he not been gunned down?

Sadat is pictured next to former Israeli prime minister Golda Meir during his monumental visit to Israel in 1977. He will be remembered for his attempts to make peace with Israel.

Sadat with Israeli prime minister Menachem Begin in 1977. This historic meeting helped erode the myth that Israelis and Arabs could never negotiate face to face.

The Ability to Lead

Anwar Sadat engineered many changes that directly affected the lives of all Egyptians. He came into office on the heels of Nasser. At that time, censorship, a secret police service, government corruption, and an ailing economy were crippling Egypt. Sadat set out to see if he could come up with something better.

And he did. According to author Thomas Lippman, Sadat "peeled this structure away layer by layer."[98] In his eleven years of rule, Anwar Sadat reenergized the economy, steering it toward a more democratic model. He oriented foreign policy away from the Soviets and toward the United States. He took the fear of war away from the Egyptians. And he

managed to gain back land from Israel that had been taken in the 1967 war—an achievement no other Arab leader had been able to match.

The Ability to Change

Anwar Sadat was an example of an individual willing to change his way of thinking and acting. He was guided by the ideas he had cultivated in Cell 54. He was especially guided by the necessity of change. As he later wrote in his memoirs, "He who cannot change the very fabric of his thought will never be able to change reality."[99]

Sadat believed an individual could indeed change reality, and throughout his life he acted on that belief. "He saw himself, in all sincerity, as a maker of history," wrote Fernandez-Armesto, "a visionary who strove, and often succeeded, to make reality of his visions despite adverse circumstances."[100]

Some scholars, though, disagree with this explanation. They claim that Sadat's achievements were a case of being in the right place at the right time and were accomplished only through improvisation and guessing, not according to a cohesive plan or vision. As Felipe Fernandez-Armesto suggests, perhaps the truth lies between the two views.

Style of Leadership

Sadat's style of leadership also earned him a place in history. He always said that his style of leadership was based on personal experience, rather than on theories or sys-

Sadat remains known as a courageous figure for his great strides in making peace with Israel. As Sadat himself once said, "Nothing in this world could rank higher than peace."

tems of politics. In leadership, he took an intuitive approach. He also recognized and freely attributed the sources of his strength to his devout faith as a Muslim, as well as to the support of his family and es-pecially his wife, Jehan.

Additionally, Anwar Sadat had a talent for using images and symbols to effect the responses of his people. He was in this way a very modern politician. Before the age of television in Egypt, the people knew their leaders only from a distance. They heard stories about them, and they might see pictures of them in the newspapers or in books.

Sadat, though, used television to a great advantage. With his televised fireside chats and other carefully planned appearances, Sadat became a real person to the Egyptians. His face was with them in the privacy of their homes. They could look into it, see the imperfections, watch the expressions change. Journalist Mohamed Heikal wrote, "He was the first Egyptian Pharaoh to come before his people armed with a camera . . ."[101] Writer Fernandez-Armesto stated that Sadat's "knowledge of the world's media and of mass communication was uncanny."[102]

Sadat achieved greatness in his life by working for peace in an area of the world known for bitter conflict and violent struggle. Some would say that in this sense, Anwar Sadat was a man ahead of his time. His wife, Jehan, has another opinion, however. "I do not agree. How can the idea of peace, of ending war, be ahead of its time?"[103]

How indeed?

Notes

Introduction: A Bold Move

1. Anwar el-Sadat, *In Search of Identity*. New York: Harper and Row, 1977.
2. Anwar el-Sadat, *In Search of Identity*.
3. Anwar el-Sadat, *In Search of Identity*.

Chapter 1: Loving the Land, Hating the Occupiers

4. George Sullivan, *Sadat: The Man Who Changed Mid-East History*. New York: Walker and Company, 1981.
5. Anwar el-Sadat, *In Search of Identity*.
6. Anwar el-Sadat, *In Search of Identity*.
7. Anwar el-Sadat, *In Search of Identity*.
8. Anwar el-Sadat, *In Search of Identity*.
9. Camelia Sadat, *My Father and I*. New York: Macmillan Publishing Company, 1985.
10. Anwar el-Sadat, *In Search of Identity*.
11. Anwar el-Sadat, *In Search of Identity*.
12. Patricia Aufderheide, *World Leaders Past and Present: Sadat*. New York: Chelsea House Publishers, Inc., 1985.
13. George Sullivan, *Sadat: The Man Who Changed Mid-East History*.

Chapter 2: Cell 54

14. Peter Woodward, *Nasser*. New York: Longman, 1992.
15. Anwar el-Sadat, *In Search of Identity*.
16. Anwar el-Sadat, *In Search of Identity*.
17. Anwar el-Sadat, *In Search of Identity*.
18. Anwar el-Sadat, *In Search of Identity*.
19. Anwar el-Sadat, *In Search of Identity*.
20. Raymond Carroll, *Anwar Sadat*. New York: Franklin Watts, 1982.
21. Raymond William Baker, *Sadat and After: Struggles for Egypt's Political Soul*. Boston: Harvard University Press, 1990.

22. Anwar el-Sadat, *In Search of Identity*.
23. Felipe Fernandez-Armesto, *Sadat and His Statecraft*. London: The Kensal Press, 1982.
24. Raymond Carroll, *Anwar Sadat*.

Chapter 3: In Nasser's Shadow

25. Raymond Carroll, *Anwar Sadat*.
26. Anwar el-Sadat, *In Search of Identity*.
27. Anwar el-Sadat, *In Search of Identity*.
28. Anwar el-Sadat, *In Search of Identity*.
29. Raymond Carroll, *Anwar Sadat*.
30. Raymond Carroll, *Anwar Sadat*.
31. Anwar el-Sadat, *In Search of Identity*.
32. Anwar el-Sadat, *In Search of Identity*.
33. Felipe Fernandez-Armesto, *Sadat and His Statecraft*.
34. George Sullivan, *Sadat: The Man Who Changed Mid-East History*.
35. George Sullivan, *Sadat: The Man Who Changed Mid-East History*.
36. George Sullivan, *Sadat: The Man Who Changed Mid-East History*.
37. George Sullivan, *Sadat: The Man Who Changed Mid-East History*.
38. George Sullivan, *Sadat: The Man Who Changed Mid-East History*.
39. Camelia Sadat, *My Father and I*.

Chapter 4: The New Leader

40. Felipe Fernandez-Armesto, *Sadat and His Statecraft*.
41. Anwar el-Sadat, *In Search of Identity*.
42. Mohamed Heikal, *Autumn of Fury: The Assassination of Sadat*. New York: Random House, 1983.
43. Raymond Carroll, *Anwar Sadat*.
44. George Sullivan, *Sadat: The Man Who Changed Mid-East History*.

45. Raymond Carroll, *Anwar Sadat.*

46. Raymond A. Hinnebusch Jr., *Egyptian Politics Under Sadat.* Cambridge: Cambridge University Press, 1985.

47. Mohamed Heikal, *Autumn of Fury: The Assassination of Sadat.*

48. George Sullivan, *Sadat: The Man Who Changed Mid-East History.*

49. Mohamed Heikal, *Autumn of Fury: The Assassination of Sadat.*

50. Mohamed Heikal, *Autumn of Fury: The Assassination of Sadat.*

51. Deborah Nodler Rosen, *Anwar el-Sadat: A Man of Peace.* Chicago: Childrens Press, 1986.

52. Mohamed Heikal, *Autumn of Fury: The Assassination of Sadat.*

53. George Sullivan, *Sadat: The Man Who Changed Mid-East History.*

Chapter 5: The October War of 1973

54. Anwar el-Sadat, *In Search of Identity.*

55. Felipe Fernandez-Armesto, *Sadat and His Statecraft.*

56. Felipe Fernandez-Armesto, *Sadat and His Statecraft.*

57. George Sullivan, *Sadat: The Man Who Changed Mid-East History.*

58. Anwar el-Sadat, *In Search of Identity.*

59. George Sullivan, *Sadat: The Man Who Changed Mid-East History.*

60. Mohamed Heikal, *Autumn of Fury: The Assassination of Sadat.*

61. Patricia Aufderheide, *World Leaders Past and Present: Sadat.*

62. Raymond Carroll, *Anwar Sadat.*

63. George Sullivan, *Sadat: The Man Who Changed Mid-East History.*

Chapter 6: Peace with Israel

64. Felipe Fernandez-Armesto, *Sadat and His Statecraft.*

65. Mohamed Heikal, *Autumn of Fury: The As-*
sassination of Sadat.

66. "Sadat's Sacred Mission," *Time*, November 28, 1977.

67. Mohamed Heikal, *Autumn of Fury: The Assassination of Sadat.*

68. Patricia Aufderheide, *World Leaders Past and Present: Sadat.*

69. Raymond Carroll, *Anwar Sadat.*

70. Raymond Carroll, *Anwar Sadat.*

71. "Sadat's Sacred Mission," *Time*, November 28, 1977.

72. Jehan Sadat, *A Woman of Egypt.* New York: Simon and Schuster, 1987.

73. Bernard Gwertzman, "Query to Jerusalem Post Writer Gave Sadat Idea for His Journey" *New York Times*, November 20, 1977.

74. Raymond Carroll, *Anwar Sadat.*

75. Raymond Carroll, *Anwar Sadat.*

76. Raymond Carroll, *Anwar Sadat.*

77. *New York Times*, November 20, 1977.

78. *New York Times*, November 20, 1977.

79. "Sadat's Sacred Mission," *Time*, November 28, 1977.

80. George Sullivan, *Sadat: The Man Who Changed Mid-East History.*

81. "Sadat's Sacred Mission," *Time*, November 28, 1977.

82. Glenn Frankel, "Bittersweet 10th Anniversary—Sadat's Visit to Israel Raised Great Hopes but Little Fulfillment," *Seattle Times*, November 20, 1987.

83. Thomas W. Lippman, *Egypt After Nasser: Sadat, Peace, and the Mirage of Prosperity.* New York: Paragon House, 1989.

84. Mohamed Heikal, *Autumn of Fury: The Assassination of Sadat.*

Chapter 7: Revolution of the Spirit

85. George Sullivan, *Sadat: The Man Who Changed Mid-East History.*

86. Jehan Sadat, *A Woman of Egypt.*

87. George Sullivan, *Sadat: The Man Who Changed Mid-East History.*

88. George Sullivan, *Sadat: The Man Who Changed Mid-East History.*

89. Felipe Fernandez-Armesto, *Sadat and His Statecraft.*

90. Thomas W. Lippman, *Egypt After Nasser: Sadat, Peace, and the Mirage of Prosperity.*

91. "An Act of Infamy," *Newsweek,* October 19, 1981.

Epilogue: A Man Ahead of His Time

92. "An Act of Infamy," *Newsweek,* October 19, 1981.

93. David Hirst and Irene Beeson, *Sadat.* London: Faber and Faber Limited, 1981.

94. "An Act of Infamy," *Newsweek,* October 19, 1981.

95. "An Act of Infamy," *Newsweek,* October 19, 1981.

96. Thomas W. Lippman, *Egypt After Nasser: Sadat, Peace, and the Mirage of Prosperity.*

97. Felipe Fernandez-Armesto, *Sadat and His Statecraft.*

98. Thomas W. Lippman, *Egypt After Nasser: Sadat, Peace, and the Mirage of Prosperity.*

99. Raymond Carroll, *Anwar Sadat.*

100. Felipe Fernandez-Armesto, *Sadat and His Statecraft.*

101. Mohamed Heikal, *Autumn of Fury: The Assassination of Sadat.*

102. Felipe Fernandez-Armesto, *Sadat and His Statecraft.*

103. Jehan Sadat, *A Woman of Egypt.*

For Further Reading

Patricia Aufderheide, *World Leaders Past and Present: Sadat.* New York: Chelsea House Publishers, Inc., 1985. A thorough account of the life of Anwar Sadat peppered with revealing quotes and a generous variety of black-and-white photos. Also features an introductory essay, "On Leadership," by Professor Arthur M. Schlesinger Jr.

Raymond William Baker, *Sadat and After: Struggles for Egypt's Political Soul.* Boston: Harvard University Press, 1990. Identifies and discusses alternate political groups in modern Egypt. Baker's in-depth coverage reveals, among other things, the contempt or respect at the fringes of Egyptian society for the Sadat era. No photos.

Raymond Carroll, *Anwar Sadat.* New York: Franklin Watts, 1982. A clear and concise portrait of the Egyptian leader as well as the political times in which he lived.

Felipe Fernandez-Armesto, *Sadat and his Statecraft.* London: The Kensal Press, 1982. A scholarly study of Sadat as a statesman. Through this detailed study of events and writings from Sadat's public and private lives, the author provides fascinating insights into the rise of Anwar Sadat, from poor villager to president of Egypt.

Mohamed Heikal, *Autumn of Fury: The Assassination of Sadat.* New York: Random House, 1983. An entertaining and controversial view of the life and assassination of Anwar Sadat by a journalist active during the rules of both Nasser and Sadat and a friend to both men. Concentrating on the life of Sadat and the plot to assassinate him, this book contains information and perspectives unavailable in other biographies. Included also is a startling black-and-white photo of the assassination.

Raymond A. Hinnebusch Jr., *Egyptian Politics Under Sadat.* Cambridge: Cambridge University Press, 1985. A thorough, scholarly look at political life in Egypt under Anwar Sadat. Serious and detail oriented.

David Hirst and Irene Beeson, *Sadat.* London: Faber and Faber Limited, 1981. A sweeping account of the Sadat years. There is generous coverage of Sadat's relationship with American statesmen (particularly Henry Kissinger) and also a comprehensive epilogue written in the wake of the assassination. No photos.

Thomas W. Lippman, *Egypt After Nasser: Sadat, Peace, and the Mirage of Prosperity.* New York: Paragon House, 1989. Valuable for its overview of Egyptian society during the Sadat years. A respected journalist and author, Lippman worked for five years at the Cairo office of the *Washington Post* and offers a well-documented and anecdotal account of a nation beset by social and economic problems, despite the international achievements of its leader.

Deborah Nodler Rosen, *Anwar el-Sadat: A Man of Peace.* Chicago: Childrens Press, 1986. Includes revealing summaries of each day of the momentous Camp David peace talks, as well as photos and a detailed chronology of the life of Anwar Sadat.

Anwar el-Sadat, *In Search of Identity*. New York: Harper and Row, 1977. In this highly personal autobiography of the Egyptian leader, Sadat reviews his life as he sees it—which does not always coincide with interpretations of historians. Nevertheless, this is the place to begin for those interested in the first Arab leader to make peace with Israel.

Camelia Sadat, *My Father and I*. New York: Macmillan Publishing Company, 1985. Anwar Sadat's daughter Camelia began writing this book after the assassination of her father. Valuable for its illustration of a complex and intimate father-daughter relationship, as well as its black-and-white photos, which reveal personal moments in the lives of members of the Sadat family.

Jehan Sadat, *A Woman of Egypt*. New York: Simon and Schuster, 1987. Jehan Sadat was married to Anwar Sadat and played an important role in her husband's day to day affairs; her book features an intimate look at the personalities and events that shaped Egypt during and immediately after her husband's rule. Valuable for its observations of the powerful people Mrs. Sadat met and dealt with in her role as first lady of Egypt.

George Sullivan, *Sadat: The Man Who Changed Mid-East History*. New York: Walker and Company, 1981. Though completed at about the time of the 1981 assassination of Sadat, George Sullivan's biography is a comprehensive introduction to the subject. The author provides in-depth coverage of military weapons and cease-fire and peace agreements, as well as important photos and document reproductions.

Peter Woodward. *Nasser*. New York: Longman, 1992. While the subject of Peter Woodward's fine biography is Sadat's predecessor, *Nasser* offers many illuminating perspectives on the political growth of Anwar Sadat in the years he served under his friend, Gamel Abdul Nasser.

Works Consulted

Raymond William Baker, *Sadat and After: Struggles for Egypt's Political Soul.* Boston: Harvard University Press, 1990.

Raymond Carroll, *Anwar Sadat.* New York: Franklin Watts, 1982.

Felipe Fernandez-Armesto, *Sadat and His Statecraft.* London: The Kensal Press, 1982.

Glenn Frankel, "Bittersweet 10th Anniversary—Sadat's Visit to Israel Raised Great Hopes but Little Fulfillment," *Seattle Times,* November 20, 1987.

Mohamed Heikal, *Autumn of Fury: The Assassination of Sadat.* New York: Random House, 1983.

Raymond A. Hinnebusch Jr., *Egyptian politics Under Sadat.* Cambridge: Cambridge University Press, 1985.

David Hirst and Irene Beeson, *Sadat.* London: Faber and Faber Limited, 1981.

Thomas W. Lippman, *Egypt After Nasser: Sadat, Peace, and the Mirage of Prosperity.* New York: Paragon House, 1989.

Newsweek, "An Act of Infamy," October 19, 1981.

Anwar el-Sadat, *In Search of Identity.* New York: Harper and Row, 1977

Camelia Sadat, *My Father and I.* New York: Macmillan Publishing Company, 1985.

Jehan Sadat, *A Woman of Egypt.* New York: Simon and Schuster, 1987.

New York Times, November 20, 1977.

Time, "Sadat's Sacred Mission," November 28, 1977.

Index

Picture Credits

Cover photo by David Hume Kennerly/ Contact Press Images Inc.

AP/Wide World Photos, 9, 23, 24, 27, 34 (bottom), 35, 36, 38, 39, 40, 42, 45 (bottom), 46, 49, 50, 55, 58, 73, 74, 75, 78, 80 (bottom), 82, 83, 84, 90, 92, 94, 98

The Bettmann Archive, 18

Bettmann/Hulton, 14, 29

Courtesy Jimmy Carter Library, 85, 86, 99

Alain Dejean/Sygma, 81

FPG, 12

Ken Lambert/FPG, 17

National Archives, 21, 22

By special permission of Jehan Sadat, 10, 20

Sygma, 57

United Nations, 60

United Nations/Y. Nagata, 70

UPI/Bettmann, 16, 26, 30, 32, 33, 34 (top), 37, 41, 43, 44 (both), 48, 51, 52, 53, 56, 61, 62, 63, 64, 65, 66, 67, 68, 71, 76, 77, 80 (top), 88, 93, 95, 96, 97

About the Author

Arthur Diamond, born in Queens, New York, received a bachelor's degree in English from the University of Oregon and a master's degree in English/Writing from Queens College.

Mr. Diamond is the author of several nonfiction books, including *The Bhopal Chemical Leak* and *Smallpox and the American Indian* in Lucent Books' World Disasters series, as well as *The Importance of Jackie Robinson*. A writer and teacher, he lives in New York with his wife Irina and their children, Benjamin Thomas and Jessica Ann.